In Our Own Voices
Learning and Teaching Toward Decolonisation

edited by Proma Tagore

Larkuma
Winnipeg, Canada

In Our Own Voices: Learning and Teaching Toward Decolonisation
Edited by Proma Tagore

Printed and bound in Canada

Canadian Cataloguing in Publication Data
In Our Own Voices: Learning and Teaching Toward Decolonisation
Proma Tagore
ISBN 0-9733821-2-0

Published in Canada

by Larkuma

720 Pasadena Avenue
Winnipeg, Manitoba
Canada R3T 2T3
larkuma2003@yahoo.com

ACKNOWLEDGEMENTS

This anthology was created with the support of many people. I am grateful, firstly, to all of the contributors - for the strength of your words and imaginings. I have been honoured to work with each and every one of you. I thank you for your hard work and for your generosity in being willing to share your stories and experiences with others.

Some very special thanks go out to Meghan Jezewska, Rubina Sidhu, Jennie Duguay, and Naomi Horii, who helped with the layout and formatting of the anthology, as well as with various other aspects of conceptualisation. Your assistance and encouragement have meant a great deal to me. I would also like to acknowledge the UVic Women's Centre, the UVic *Thirdspace* collective, the UVic Students of Colour Collective, and CFUV Radio for their support, feedback, enthusiasm, and for letting out the word on the anthology.

Many, many thanks to Olivia Ashbee, for helping me to dream up this project, for hours of invaluable assistance with the editorial process, help with layout, for discussing all aspects of the anthology with me, and more generally for your daily support, love, laughter, and care.

I would also like to express my gratitude to my family – especially to my mother, Bashori Tagore, and my father, Prasun Tagore – for your support throughout my education and in all that I do. To my sister, Shaunga – I am grateful for our conversations and for your presence more generally. I am truly honoured to be able to include your writing as part of this work.

Thank you to Uma Parameswaran for taking on the project of publishing this anthology, and for all the ways you have empowered women of colour writers inside and outside the academy for so many years.

Thank you also to the Learning and Teaching Centre at the University of Victoria for providing funds and much valuable support for this project.

I have been incredibly lucky to work over the past few years with some very brave, daring, hard-working, and inspiring students while teaching here at the University of Victoria. Thank you for making my experience of teaching/learning a meaningful one. This book is dedicated to you.

A couple of the pieces in this anthology have been previously published in other venues, and I would like to acknowledge these. njeri-damali (campbell)'s essay was first published in *Canadian Woman Studies/les cahiers de la femme* 23.2 (Winter 2004) issue on 'Women and the Black Diaspora', and is reprinted with permission. Michelle La Flamme's essay was originally published in *Thirdspace: The Journal for Emerging Feminist Scholars* 3.1 (November, 2003), and I gratefully acknowledge permission to reprint this as well.

TABLE OF CONTENTS

Introduction

Learning and Teaching for Decolonisation

Proma Tagore

The struggle of marginalised peoples to set the terms through which we define, understand, and express our selves has been a crucial and recurrent theme in anti-racist activism, in movements for decolonisation, independence, or self-determination, and in social justice movements more generally. The title of this anthology, *In Our Own Voices*, is meant to invoke this desire and this insistence: that we, as marginalised people, have the right to name our own experiences, to claim our own knowledges, and to speak our own stories, as opposed to having others speak for us, describe our realities to us, or produce knowledge about us.

Taking this basic principle as a starting point, this anthology examines, more specifically, the question of what it means to teach, learn, or undertake projects relating to knowledge, consciousness, pedagogy, and education with the goals of decolonisation, anti-racism, or anti-oppressive struggle and practice. The desire for a collected volume of work by students, teachers, activists and others committed to challenging racism and colonialism in their work grew directly out of my own experiences teaching as a queer woman of colour in a predominantly white, Eurocentric institutional setting – and the various issues, difficulties, and questions that such a positioning entails. This anthology was created with the intention that it could serve at once as a practical guide that might help marginalised students and staff better negotiate their educational experiences, as a place where we could find ourselves and our stories reflected, as a means of sharing our knowledges, and as an entry-point for identifying strategies of resistance that could make a difference to our university campuses or to our learning more broadly.

As I reflect on my own experiences as both a student, and now also an instructor of 'postcolonial literature' within the context of the Department of English at the University of Victoria, I cannot avoid being reminded of the political and historical links between the institutions in which I am situated and the trajectories of British imperialism. Similarly, my placement and faltering belongings in this institutional setting are unequivocally bound up with a variety of other stories that I could tell about myself – stories having to do with histories of immigration; experiences of racism and racialisation; my class and caste positionings; my inconsistent and awkward relationships with both the English and Bengali languages; the things I remember and forget; how I live my gender and sexuality; my understandings of family, home and community; or my passion for and sense of survival through various acts of storytelling – all related to my particular placement in global histories of colonisation and capitalism. My different embodiments in systems of privilege and subordination, and consequently in the space of the classroom or university, necessarily pose various challenges, questions, contradictions and dilemmas that require me to reflect on, critique, historicise, and politicise my teaching and learning in such spaces.

Historically in the west, the university is a space that has been reserved for the white middle-class – a fact that is reflected not only in its culture, but also in its curriculum and the ways in which it conceives of both knowledge and instruction. With the growing pressures effected by the numerous anti-colonial resistances and claims for Indigenous rights that have taken place around the world, and due to the impact of related social movements such as the US Civil Rights movement, feminism, and gay and lesbian rights movements, small spaces have been opened up within North American universities for some demographic shifts along the lines of class, gender, race, and sexual orientation. Yet, even as 'minority groups' begin to occupy different sites within Canadian and US academic institutions, and even as there is now a growing body of intellectual work on issues of race, gender, sexuality, class and colonialism, the basic structures and functioning of university life – including curriculum, pedagogy, or resources and support for marginalised students and faculty – remain largely unchanged. Marginalised students and staff still typically 'fall through the cracks' of such institutions, with little support.

Students of colour and First Nations students face particular problems negotiating classrooms and the university in general. Some of the daily issues faced by these students include: a general silence around colonialism, racism, and racialised experiences; backlash for speaking up against racism; isolation in classes and within departments; racist violence, harassment and threat; a Eurocentric curriculum and the absence of voices and histories that speak to the realities, knowledges, and needs of people of colour and Indigenous people; stereotyping, silencing, marginalisation, invisibility, tokenism and/or objectification in classrooms both by other students and by white professors; a lack of models and/or resources to help manoeuvre specific circumstances, including seeking redress for harassment, coping with racism, or imagining anti-colonial and anti-racist spaces and methods of learning; a lack of supervision, support and/or expertise for projects on anti-racism or on histories and knowledges developed outside, apart from, or in resistance to colonial ways of knowing.

Indeed, the context of most North American universities is still one in which non-white histories and realities are often absented or else 'othered' – that is, presented from the perspective of white hegemony. A great deal of what is deemed to be valuable knowledge by the university thus neither resonates nor has much theoretical/practical meaning and relevance in the context of the lives of Indigenous people and people of colour. Colonialism and racism, including the systemic ways in which knowledge is racialised by the institution, deeply affect and mediate how experiences of learning and university education are structured for these marginalised students.

This anthology came out of a direct need for a resource that could help racialised students to better negotiate their educational experiences and, along with others, create ways of resisting racism on campuses, in classrooms, and in class materials. The call for papers for this anthology was inspired by the words of June Jordan, the African-American poet, educator, and activist, who wrote: "For us, there is nothing optional about 'black experience' and/or 'black studies': we must know ourselves."[1] Indeed, one of the recurrent sentiments expressed to me by both marginalised students and faculty in the institution at which I currently teach is of the crucial role played by fora where individuals are able to know and reflect on the stories and experiences of others located in similar sorts of positions, especially as these positionings are so often marked by and through isolation. Sometimes, hypocritically, there is a great deal of pressure from the white administration for the few racialised individuals and groups who are situated within the university to 'teach anti-racism', to take on the sole responsibility for developing anti-racist curricula, for placing issues related to racism and colonialism on the university's agenda, to educate racist white professors and administrators about their own racisms – or to somehow, magically, in the framework of the one hour that has been reserved for a single workshop on anti-racism, or more probably on 'diversity', do away with racism once and for all at the university. I have come to recognise these demands less as indicators of an honest, committed, or authentic readiness to work toward a more socially just environment, and more as acts of denial: ways of trivialising the realities of racism in the lives of people of colour and Indigenous people, and of silencing or containing ongoing discussions of colonialism and race. This anthology was created with the idea that it is important to ask questions about who is asked to bear the responsibility for undoing racism and colonisation, and who is absolved from having to think through one's own implication within multiple and interlocking systems of power, privilege, and oppression. I think, in many ways, the poetry, essays, and artwork included in this anthology are not all that interested in 'educating others'; rather, this work is about having conversations with one another, knowing ourselves better, and through this, developing new imaginings for how we might organise our resistances more effectively.

While many of the issues covered in this anthology relate specifically and directly to university education, it must be noted that experiences of silencing, invisibility, and violence for people of colour and Indigenous people are by no means unique to the university setting. These experiences are part of our daily living. As Rubina Sidhu writes in her essay that is included in this anthology, the feeling of marginality, in conjunction with the need to undo and resist this marginalisation through anti-racist education and practice, is a struggle that "goes far beyond the classroom; it goes into the corners of everything I do."[2] The university is thus one institution that functions in combination with other colonial institutions – including western law; government; institutions of modern science and medicine; white Christianity, including Christian missionisation; institutions that regulate families and sexualities; business; the military; social services; and schooling more generally – to uphold systems of colonial and racial domination. The racism that we, as people of colour, might face in the context of North American classrooms and universities must therefore be located within this broader framework of global and local, institutional and everyday forms of racial violence, domination, and subjugation.

When I walk into my classrooms, I do not and cannot simply leave these relations behind me, at the door. When I walk into a classroom and into the university, I am profoundly reminded that many of us who are here, indeed if we find ourselves here at all, do not enter on equal terms. In asking myself what it means to teach and learn toward decolonisation, I make an effort to be accountable to such institutional positionings, while also striving to shift these relations. I do this in an attempt to move beyond and outside of certain colonial frameworks of teaching, learning, and knowing, and toward being able to see and speak myself more clearly, more wholly, more truthfully, and through terms of my own making.

While this work draws from, and is inspired by, an established and growing body of writing on issues of anti-racist and anti-oppressive education and pedagogy, I feel that this anthology is unique in the extent to which it centres the voices, narratives, writing, and perspectives of students, in particular. For both the contributors to, and readers of, this anthology, I hope that the various narratives included herein will offer all of us ways to think through institutional experiences that are often constructed as isolated ones and, instead, through shared reflections, reconstruct these experiences and our educational projects in ways that are liberatory and empowering.

Notes

1. June Jordan, cited in Chandra Mohanty, *Feminism Without Borders* (Durham: Duke UP, 2003), 197.
2. Rubina Sidhu, "Blankets of Silence," *In Our Own Voices,* ed. Proma Tagore (Winnipeg: Larkuma, 2005).

a/li(f)ve to tell

njeri-damali (campbell)

aftereffects: njeri-damali (campbell)

photo credit: Babatunde Martins, 2002

My mere existence in the academic world challenges colonialism. The fact that i write like this, sing like this, breathe like this, or breathe at all, goes against a larger colonial project bent on my erasure.[1] Is this a little too harsh? Maybe it is. Maybe i'm overreacting, but i don't think so. The tears tell me otherwise.

July 15, 2003

dear mom,

it's getting darker, and i'm still at work, thinking about what i'm doing in my academic career, wondering how to really answer the question that you ask me all the time "what about your future?" i thought i'd take this opportunity to tell you a little about where i am in the world these days, and what my work is all about.

you know that i studied Political Science and Sociology in my undergrad at York. i graduated with honours, and took a year off to start my position at the Ontario Young People's Alliance. during that year, i applied for a variety of graduate programs, and was invited to study education at York, in a program called "Language, Culture, and Teaching." this continues to be a huge challenge for me, because as i progress in my studies, i realise that the work that i do is quite intense, and extremely important to me.

When i was younger, being 'self-conscious' was a bad thing. It meant, and often felt, as if the world was looking angrily over my shoulder, breathing down my neck, judging me. i've chosen to dodge that trigger, and think of myself as self-reflexive. This means that i operate with the assumption that nothing that i write, or that i produce, or that i research will ever be disconnected from me. This, by extension, now means that i start from i. i declare that my place in the world is impacted by the matrices of my identity. i am young, Black, queer, middle-classed, diasporic, university-educated, able-bodied, sex-positive, natural-haired, dark-skinned, 'heterosexy', and, and, and... i understand the world in this way. The stories that i search for, and the stories that i seek will always be anchored by this reality; i am driven by this. 'it' – the work that i produce – becomes me.

i have chosen to turn my critical gaze toward a system (the school system) that i struggled in, and was rewarded by. you and dad saw the side of school that others did. you saw my report cards which were usually pretty good, you saw me go to summer school, and then be employed at summer school. you witnessed the awards, the speeches, the special attention, and the scholarships. and many others did too: our fellow church families, our neighbours and family friends, even some of my own teachers. you saw all this, and celebrated it with me, and for that i thank you.

but there was so much more than that. i remember my grade 3 teacher, who had bright red hair and pale white skin. she seemed so tall back then. she was from Ireland, i think. anyway, she had a program called student of the month, and in this program, one student was chosen each month, based on something special they did, or their marks, or something. the winning student each month would get their name put up on the board, along with a photograph. gold and red stars would be festooned around their face, and they would also get a nice certificate.

i wanted, more than anything, to be student of the month. it was the last full month of school – may – my birth month. and some of my classmates had told me that i would probably be chosen. i kept my hopes up... the first few days of may passed by, and no student was chosen! 'why?' i wondered.. i thought maybe she had stopped early this year, or maybe she was still deciding who to pick. one whole week passed by, and another, and another... no choice was made. someone asked her one day in class, "mi-iss?" the student said, with her hand up high, "who's the student of the month?" the class fell silent, eager to hear her response.

"Njeri Campbell" our teacher responded simply, and returned to her work.

i was devastated. i had been chosen as student of the month? and she waited three weeks to put it up on the board? why didn't she celebrate me like the others?

a few days after, the school was dismissed for the holidays, and i, embarrassed, left the class, sadder than ever. i would have preferred not being chosen, over this sorry state of affairs.

this wasn't the first such event, and was definitely not the last. i came up against school, as an institution in so many ways. often when i made complaints, or explained my situations, i was told not to be so sensitive, by you and dad; or i was told that nothing could be done, by the authority figures at the school.

that was a difficult experience to deal with, and as a result i generated a very violent anger toward my teachers which resulted in many conflicts. when i switched schools, and i went to St. Andrews' french immersion program, things got even worse. i had decided to shift my identity, and symbolised that shift by changing the pronunciation of my name. "Na-je-raye" i told people to call me, and Na-je-raye i became. Na-je-raye was funny, the new girl in class, not so good in french but very good in english. Na-je-raye, was rich. although she lived in a lower-income, working class part of the city, she told people that her family was rich, that she had a butler, and many limousines.

at first, people believed her, and many of the students around her wanted to be her friend. but, little by little, the other girls at school found her out, and cornered her in the yard one day after class.

i remember that day very well.

i'm still pulling away from the colony, you know? Some writers (i don't know their names) talk about the theory of a 'colonized mind', which i think refers to those who were done in by the colonial project, who no longer need a person, or institution to colonize them, because they have perfected the art on their own. Sometimes i ask myself if i can escape this ever. Even though i do share who i am and where i am placed, i still come from a world that has made secret deposits into my life account whenever i have played their game. At times, i feel as if it is not enough to play the identity game, and out myself. i must do more.

These days, 'more' means re-membering; bringing/drudging/yanking/coaxing stuff up from the past and looking at it again, re-telling the tales, re-singing the songs, and grounding through/with it. I have learned lately, that this work can be called 'oral history' or 'ethnographic re-search'. It is pretty messy and is described by Fern Ingersoll and Jasper Ingersoll as "... a continuous, night- and- day series of happenings, plots thickening and thinning, information flowing in all directions, and insights coaxed out of the confusion."[2] It is messy. In its mental aspect, it means frenzied notes, unfinished sentences, digging up the past, and learning what others have said about it. Emotionally, it means redemptive giggles, feelings of release/repress/release, it means hope and doubt, shame and fear, triumph and always, always risk. Physically, it means torrents of shivers, rage, tentative eye-contact or bold-faced stares, yelling and silence. Tight muscles. In spirit, it means movement, healing, growth, and passage.

the ringleader came up to me and said: "we know that you're a liar, why do you say all this stuff that's not true?" i feigned as if i didn't know what she was talking about. i felt my lunch coming back up my throat and my knees were buckling. i continued to shiver in fear, and the girls closed in on me and proceeded to tell me every lie i had ever told them, from the most 'innocent' to the most elaborate of them all. i was very embarrassed, and finally i gave in and told them that they were most correct. immediately after that confession, one girl stepped up from the group and said that they had all decided to forgive me, as long as i vowed never to lie again. i promised them all that i wouldn't, and that i would do my best to undo the wrongs i had done.

Do i dare to tell the truths again? When i think of defending my work, i think of this memory. Do i continue to produce the work that i do? Work in which i change the margins, play with ideas, become vulnerable on paper? Should i? Is this the right anti-colonial project for me right now? Can it backfire? Cynthia Tyson declares that emancipatory researchers (like myself?) "ask ourselves 'Who really benefits?'" from our work.[3] When i ask this question to myself, my answers are fewer than expected. As a graduate student, my work is created alone, and is sometimes read by my partner and/or friends while it's being created.[4] At this point it is handed in to another who reads it, grades it, and then gives it back to me. Some years ago, i started to bind my work and bring it with me to parties, asking community members to read it, and comment on it. i have considered making a zine out of my work and distributing it to an activist community in the city, or publishing it somewhere. Maybe, i wonder, people will be moved by what i have to say, and will create and distribute, too! Does that then mean that a community will benefit from my work? Perhaps.

i walked home that evening alone, but free. i felt, for the first time, that a group of girls – a group of girls that i tried so hard to befriend – saw me for who i was, and chose to love the truth of me. i didn't have to pretend anymore.

that group of girls became my clique, and i, the photographer of the elementary unit, became their herstorian. remember that 110 camera i won at the church bazaar? with that camera, i captured so many moments at school. i tried out for the volleyball and basketball teams, but i didn't make it... i tried out for the cross country team and didn't make the quarter finals, but i got to go to the track meet and (of course) take pictures of all the cool athletes. the only success i had was in W5H: the team of smart students who would battle against other schools, asking each other skill-testing questions. we were a pretty good team, and i had a lot of fun, although it was scary, and the boys on the team were slightly aggressive and sometimes downright mean.

the teachers were okay, except when my french immersion teacher threw chalk at me and bruised my collar bone, and when they always sat me in the back row of the class, or when i was denied access to elective courses, or special events at school.

the other students knew what was happening, but they remained quiet, and i remained alone - trying to be healthy, trying to have friends, and trying to be cool.

luckily, throughout all this drama, there was a church community of elders who, in their own ways, supported my growth and development. they liked me, and supported my accomplishments. i especially liked the families who chose not to put me in competition with their children by telling them that they should be more like me.

finally, grade eight came, and thanks to you and dad fighting for me, i was placed in the advanced stream. i could go on to university after high school.

high school was more of the same in some ways, but a little bit harder. i found the school work quite easy (i still have my notes and stuff :)), and the teachers seemed pretty happy to have me there. for most of grade nine, i hung around with some friends from elementary school, and i made friends with the gifted teacher, the guidance counselor, and my math teacher. i had those huge, black, owl-like glasses that were crooked, and i didn't really think i was particularly attractive. people laughed and me and called me ugly a lot. i really wanted to have my hair braided with extensions.

anyways, i got good marks, joined the student council, and created a new position there. i quickly became known as i started creating space for myself to speak on the morning announcements (people really liked my voice), and i began contributing to the social activities of the school. grade ten came and went with one of my more intense student/teacher relationships. i challenged my teachers because i was completely fascinated by them. i wanted to know about their lives, what brought them to teaching, what made them an expert. i 'complained' a lot, and most of my teachers found me unbearable. i got mad at my history teacher for not teaching about natives, my English teacher for making us read shakespeare, our french teacher for not telling me the truth about 'the algiers', and so much just went completely out of whack.

i am often reminded that this work, the work i did, the work i do, and that my dreams, are painfully overdue ...

"[The work] is certainly not useless, but often late."[5]

...even when i felt on the cutting edge.

i soon became known for my 'arrogant' questioning nature, and my temper tantrums. in my social studies class, when my teacher walked up to my desk and slid all my belongings off of it because i hadn't cleared them away fast enough for my test, i walked out of class and slammed the door so hard the glass shattered. i did the same when a teacher gave me a low grade on a project about Egypt when the class decided it was the best mark in the class. on both occasions, i went straight down to the principal's office, and then to the guidance office to cry, and yell. and it worked.

did you know about any of this?

i'll continue to tell the stories, though. For now, that is the only way that my work can breathe. i must tell the stories, starting with my own. For now, that is the only way that my work can bleed. i must tell the stories starting with my own. Horacio N. Roque Ramírez speaks, and says that:

> Ironically, death and loss in community oral history projects allow others to come alive: in the voids left behind by the missing, the living taking their place, often with fear, often with pride and determination to speak on their behalf, to re-place in history.[6]

i have died, and re-born many times. i have lost, and loosed, and have hovered in the places where there was nothing but silence. The challenge to the colonial comes when i survive, and thrive, and – as Madonna croons – "Hope I live to tell the secrets I have learned, till then, it will burn inside of me..."[7]

burning, yes.

grade eleven changed everything.

This burning changes the world, and it is the redemption. By choosing to go back into my memory, and creating spaces where others can do the same, i/you/we resist the colonial project. We not only heal, but we make waves: creating "a larger cumulative social effect in changing the conditions..." around us.[8]

i began the youth council, started the tv show, started attending many many leadership conferences, got chosen to represent the school, and 'discovered' boys. that's when i permed my hair again and got contact lenses. the school kilt got shorter, and the navy blue tights of my uniform were exchanged for knee high socks. the lipsticks came in dark raspberry and sometimes ginger, the eyes lined in bonne bell's smoky kohl, and i wore cloë every day.

i was hot. the boys, some girls, and some teachers sensed the change in my ways, and attention came like crazy. i was smart, pretty, popular, funny, and had a bad temper. i knew my way around the classroom, and the school. i knew how to get into and out of things, and i knew what was worth the struggle and what wasn't. the freedom was incredible.

i started to hear rumours about me. the teachers didn't like me, and the students in my grade thought i was a snob. i had two or three friends throughout high school, but i didn't really have the time to give the time of day to anyone. i stopped working in groups for project work. i couldn't meet up with people because of my after school meetings, or my shoots for the tv show i ran. i was fast-paced, forward-looking, confident-seeming, aloof.

i ran for student council president and lost. people laughed at what (i have recently been told) was the most embarrassing election speech ever. i dressed up as a clown, no one laughed. i felt awful... anyways...

grade 12 and 13 went by with more of the same. things started to calm down, and my life shifted away from a school that i didn't feel a part of. on some occasions, students and teachers colluded with each other to sabotage my attempts at projects and school programming. people were tired of Na-je-raye. and, in some ways, i was too.

The Dilemmas:

- passion
- fatigue
- fear
- holding my story over others
- playing the game
- the quest for validation

i was happy to leave though, and to enter York: my next playground.

first year was great. i joined a lot of groups, like the Women's Centre, the NDP, and the Catholic Student Centre (church every day, remember?). my classes were tough, with all the reading and writing, and feelings of non-confidence in my writing. i had some great teacher assistants who taught me more about writing in their 5-minute post-classroom chats than any of my high school english teachers did. i was independent.

in second year, i dropped the Catholic Centre and the Women's Centre and started, instead, to meditate on my own. i developed a language about my own sexuality as i started meeting other people with whom i could talk to about my attractions to wimmin. my classes became more interesting. i ran for school board trustee in our city, and i kept up a good average. i became president of a campus group, and i joined student government. i also drank my first pint of beer – and enjoyed it.

i took on the name "Na-je-ree," as you named me. it took a while for people to notice the shift and then to honour it, but it came soon enough, and everyone knew. it was nice having people call me what you and dad called me at home. it was a release of a self that i had grown impatient with, a coming home, a re:birthing.

then i met Njeri, my first namesake sistah friend. we both changed our names again to the current pronunciation, one that you do not use: 'in-jeri'. i started to write my name in lower-case, and to put the 'campbell' in brackets to honour your line, the strachans.

although i enjoyed the freedom i had to write, i detested the reading i had to do and how most of the readings i read in political science – even the courses that were supposed to be about Black people – were white. that was a hard pill to swallow, and my rage continued to boil as i re-turned to those high school days of leaving classes enraged. i met with many of my professors (another trait which remained), trying and hoping against hope that they would give me something to trust, and often i was successful. professors, i found, were more willing to 'give' than teachers in my previous schools.

i visited some of my profs, got closer with my fellow classmates, and wrote some great stuff. sometimes it took a while to get my papers done, but i was creative, fun, and resourceful.

the last few years of university saw more classes, more friends, more loves, and more angst, as i wondered what my next steps would be. i put on hold my desire to apply for law school, and focused on getting things to think and write about for my graduate studies.

my undergrad ended in a touching graduation ceremony. you and dad attended, and, unbeknownst to you, so did my first woman lover. she wore a beautiful red wrap, black sunglasses and gold shoes. she stood up when my name was called. you and dad and auntie joan yelled for me. i smiled at all of you, and felt loved, and supported.

it was an afternoon of possibility, accomplishment, movement. it prepared me to be here, writing to you about this journey that i've taken, and continue to take. it prepared me for the joy and pain of grad school, the excitement of creating and finishing work, the joy of sharing laughter and tears with those who facilitate my learning, the constant breaking of my heart in these dreary hallways, the happiness that it will soon shift to something, somewhere else.

i came out, and then i moved out, and i had more space than i ever had before.

when i look ahead, i see marie and me, studying and doing our PhDs together. loving each other, against the grain, and against your wishes. i will one day teach students to teach, challenge them to tell their stories, to tell the tales of their shadowlands like i do. i will encourage them to seek redemption in the hallways, and to love hard, to love always.

last month, when we went to see that play about Nelson Rohihlahla Mandela, and little Nelson was going to leave his village forever, his mother said: "look back!! LOOK BACK!!"

you have said the same thing to me, mom. you challenge me to cherish and remember. and i do. i awaken those memories, and i put together the pieces of my own past: little bits like this letter to you, little bits through song, and photograph, little bits like tears and glances, little bits.

little bits...

"Write a final essay in which you explore how a self-conscious researcher can produce knowledge that challenges colonialism. Can research be conducted in a manner that is not 'colonial'? Draw on course readings to write this essay. Be sure to define your terms and explain any dilemmas you may encounter based on your own social/cultural characteristics (e.g. race, ethnicity, language ability, class, gender, etc.)."[9]

thank you, again, for giving birth to me.

your daughter,
njeri-damali (campbell)

Notes

1. In her discussion of the ethnocentrism that often befalls western feminist researchers, Shulamit Reinharz reminds me that through the misrepresentation of the stories of 'Other' wimmin, like myself, and through the 'projection' of Western (White, middle-class, capitalist and, and, and) values and understandings, stories like my own are whittled away. She speaks of this 'erasure' on page 120 and 121 of her essay, "Feminist Cross-Cultural Research," in *Feminist Methods in Social Research* (New York: Oxford University Press, 1992), 109-125 and 305-308.
2. Fern and Jasper Ingersoll, "Both a Borrower and a Lender Be: Ethnography, Oral History, and Grounded Theory," *Oral History Review* 15 (Spring 1987): 81-102. The quote can be found on page 91, as part of an explanation of how theory is often emergent during ethnographic practices. This 'grounded theory', characterises theory as something active, something that can be performed, and created.
3. Cynthia Tyson, "Research, Race and an Epistemology of Emancipation," *Interrogating Racism in Qualitative Research Methodology*, eds. Gerardo R. Lopez and Laurence Parker, in *Counterpoints*, volume 195 (New York, 2003): 19-28. She argues this point on page 23, where she challenges the emancipatory researcher to 'create emancipatory epistemologies from which liberator methodologies are born': *you njeri, she might whisper, you must create new ways of knowing ... so that others among you, and you yourself, can create new ways of doing. and*

as we know, and do in emancipatory ways, we challenge oppression; we change the world.
4. marie-jolie rwigema says: "like when you hear the truth of something, it resonates more deeply .. when you're living by the colonial dictate you tend to feel unsettled, but when you hear something that's true, that's true to your soul, it resonates and shifts stuff, much more profoundly. it shifts what was there before, in a way that it can't come back," phone conversation, reprinted with permission, July 18, 2003.
5. Horacio Roque Ramírez, "My Community, My History, My Practice," *Oral History Review* 29.2 (Summer/Fall):71-87. Our work is 'often late', he says, on page 89, '... certainly not useless, but often late.'
6. This is from the same article as above, on page 89.
7."Live to tell" written by Madonna and Pat Leonard (1985).
8. Elizabeth Crespo, "Puerto Rican Women: Migration and Changes in Gender Roles," *International Yearbook of Oral History*, 137-50.
9. These are the instructions for this project, written by Julia E. Curry-Rodriguez, for the (De)colonizing Research Methodologies course, Summer 2003, York University, Faculty of Education.

Selected Poems

Chiinuuks

Where there is Story, there is truth

Truth unfolds in Night Sky's lap
a Star blanket –
she spreads it carefully,
smooths out folds with translucent hands.
Spider Woman's silken thread
sewn into patches, stories,
details woven intricately.
She nods at Sun as he passes,
getting down to work,
she mends stories,
binds them with honesty,
revealing Truth.
Truth is a Star Blanket,
look to the stars and you will see
a story there
of you and me.

Freedom?

information and too much illusion,
twisted realities existing in frailties,
we negotiate our way
through consumer induced
addiction produced choices,
bodies moving within legally constructed confines,
to be produced, reduced,
reordered, cut apart, regimented and regulated
body parts strewn across concrete floors,
are we truly free?

Decolonization: Effects and Defects

past hurts and future doubts
poke at my interior
shaking the foundation of my values
We are not a ladder of people
To be forced upward emptyhanded (Chiinuuks, 2004)

hands hold my belly
attempt to contain
spilling gut, blood and intestines
full of doubt
We know who we are and where we come from
(chief Mike Maquinna, Ha'wiih 2003)

blood drains and pale-faced
I rock my swollen belly,
blood and intestines growing
back and forth, back and forth
mourning spillage

moaning gives way to Song
holding, rocking my draining belly is the dance
Hooo wai, hoo wai ! *(be careful)*
And sea serpent turned one head towards the other and saw it's black, ugly stink and said, Yes, yes this is who I have become (Kwa'wakwa story)

song releases blood and rot
rocking slows, shifts
movement induces freedom
words form under lightened tongue
finding a way out for *miaathlii (bad energy)*
riding on the backs of letters
they go popping, cracking, dead air
Hold your head up, you never look down, this is what my mother said,
Call it what it is cousin, call it what it is, name it (Ron Martin, 1999)

I let go my belly
my belly button goes back
goes back,
finding a place to rest
a reminder that just behind it
is my *tliimuxdii.*

On the Outside Looking In:

Voice, Identity and Difference in Women's Studies

Lisa Okada

When those who have the power to name and to socially construct reality choose not to see you or hear you, whether you are a dark-skinned, old, disabled, female, or speak with a different accent or dialect than theirs, when someone with the authority of a teacher, say, describes the world to you and you are not in it, there is a moment of psychic disequilibrium, as if you looked in the mirror and saw nothing.

– Adrienne Rich[1]

Introduction

I am a fourth generation Japanese Canadian woman. I was born and raised in a society where my participation, culture, community and history have been largely unrecognized. The way in which the world is presented to me, for example through television, literature, cinema and textbooks, does not reflect my reality, experience and identity. These entities profoundly shape my sense of racialised identity and understanding of 'difference'.[2] There was a time in my life when I made numerous attempts to reject my culture and silence my voice; I tried to become invisible.

Enrolling in Women's Studies was driven by my desire to see myself reflected back; I wanted to see an image mirroring my reality. Through Women's Studies, I was challenged to see my 'difference' and to situate 'difference' as produced within power, inequality and the struggle for meaning. Women's Studies forcefully asked me to critically engage how racialised identities are historically and socially produced in and outside the classroom.

Although these theories have challenged me to examine and explore who I am, it has not been a simple straightforward process. Coming to the university with a limited understanding of my own history and of power, I assumed that all Women's Studies students entered the classroom on equal footing. Because of this, I was under the impression that the Women's Studies classroom would be egalitarian, empowering and liberatory for all. I failed to see how the white western feminist project had obfuscated the complexities of 'race', class and sexuality. In fact, my experiences did not fall under the category of the universal 'woman' that this feminist agenda was projecting.

I soon discovered the truth of Roxanna Ng's assertion that "[t]he social structure of inequality on the basis of class, gender, race, ability and so on, leaks into and becomes integral to everyday life in the academy [which] means that we do not participate in the academy as equals."[3] It is from this understanding that I began to make sense of my contradictory experiences in Women's Studies: experiences that have been simultaneously empowering and disempowering.

In the Women's Studies classroom, I was conditioned to believe that I entered a space accorded to 'the other',[4] because in subtle and overt ways, I was continually reminded of my 'difference'. It was a struggle to have my voice heard, often to the extent that I was an observer rather than a participant. In other words, I could not assume a sense of 'belonging'. My realities, concerns, history and identity were, to some degree, rendered invisible in Women's Studies.

All in all, I felt that I occupied a separate sphere of realities and experiences than my classmates did. As a result, I began to question whether these experiences were unique to me or whether they were common to others as well.

Beginning with Women's Studies: A Site of Inquiry

Women's Studies in its many forms – as a radical educational approach, as a theory, and as a practice – has been instrumental in challenging dominant methods of education. It provides a space for theorizing and understanding systems that impact women and marginalised peoples. In terms of scholarship and practice, feminism and Women's Studies direct attention to racism more so than do other disciplines. It plays a significant role in placing racism on the agenda as legitimate grounds for theorizing, organizing and social change. However, as relations in the classroom play out, it becomes apparent that Women's Studies classrooms are not exempt from practices of racism and classism. Women's relationships and experiences are certainly shaped by these conditions, and the classroom can be a stage upon which racialised women students participate, interact and discover the disappearance of their experience, histories and stories.

Day-to-day interactions reproduce relations of domination and subordination in the classroom for racialised women students. For example, familiar constructions such as the notion of 'Third World women' as backward, or as culture- and tradition-bound, discursively reproduce common conceptions of 'otherness'. Popular ideas of 'otherness' circulate in the classroom to fix and position racialised people and take away their agency. Racialised students must continually challenge and redefine their experience/identities beyond these constructions.

Given these experiences, I began to ask myself this question: in what ways are my experiences as a racialised woman student similar and/or different from the experiences of other racialised students in Women's Studies classes?[5] In beginning to answer this question, it must be made clear that my intent is not to place blame or responsibility on faculty, students or the department of Women's Studies, nor do I want to represent myself or the women that participated in my research as victims.[6] Rather, I hope to see how our experiences operate within power structures that produce and perpetuate 'difference'.

Voice in the Classroom – Storytelling/Silences/Authority

Voice, especially how it plays out in the classroom, is a critical factor in the experiences of racialised women in classroom situations. Issues of voice in the classroom are imbricated with complex dynamics between speaker and listener.

Trinh T. Minh-ha's concept of 'specialness' is useful in thinking about how racialised voices are mediated, heard and/or silenced in classrooms. Minh-ha uses the concept of 'specialness' to describe how racialised subjects are 'othered', and how certain meanings of 'otherness' are carried into class discussions, course material and interactions between students.[7] Constructions of racialised people within the discourse of 'specialness', as Minh-ha explains it, function to sustain the dominant's gaze, as socially dominant groups commodify, romanticize, appropriate and objectify the voices, narratives and experiences of racialised people. 'Specialness' translates into entertainment for the dominant social group, and stems from their desire to 'spice up' their lives. This culture of domination is preserved through the gaze: racialised students speak, white students listen and learn. Racialised students, then, are sought after by virtue of their irreconcilable and inescapable 'visibility'. Thus, while it may seem that racialised students can be regarded as speaking subjects in the classroom, what is and is not permissible in terms of the content of their speech is equally important in considering how these students are silenced, as well as how their identities are constructed, categorically, within the classroom. This superficial and contingent granting of space is what marks racialised minority students' speech as 'special' in spaces that are predominantly white.

The role of the audience, and the context that informs these dynamics (dynamics which can potentially result in silence and little or no participation) are also crucial in understanding how voice functions in the classroom. It is also important to examine the role of the racialised student speaker who may internalize expectations for authentic stories.

We Speak Back: Silence and the Lack of Representation[8]

> Speaking out is not a simple gesture of freedom in a culture of domination... There would be no need to even speak of the oppressed and exploited coming to voice, articulating and redefining reality, if there were no oppressive mechanisms of silencing, suppressing, and censoring.
>
> – bell hooks[9]

Through talking with other racialised students in Women's Studies, it became clear that we all shared experiences of silencing in the classroom.[10] We identified power and marginality as dimensions that inhibit speaking. Furthermore, Women's Studies discourse and philosophy emits the illusion that its classrooms are premised on free-speech and equal opportunity, and we were not prepared or equipped to deal with our own silence in these classrooms. Interestingly, instead of examining the actual conditions of the classroom that shaped how/when/why we speak, some of us had become self-critical.

Silencing within classrooms operates in a variety of different ways. Silence, on the part of racialised students, stems from our fears about miscommunication, our fear of being 'read' incorrectly by classmates, or from fears around being interpreted as emotional, reactionary or irrational when speaking about issues of racialisation. For examplc, in the following excerpt, 'Santa Maria' discusses her experiences and feelings of vulnerability about her words being reduced or dismissed in accordance to circulating constructions of women of colour:

> And I know that I don't want to be branded as angry, although I know that I am. I mean all of what I have said, I speak because I am angry but I don't want my speaking to be reduced to an emotional response. I don't want that.

Speaking about personal issues entails vulnerability. Some of us fall into silence because of our feelings of inadequacy or an inability to display confidence to speak in the classroom. The idea of 'putting yourself out there', or of speaking to issues that do not correspond with that of the majority, makes speaking increasingly difficult. Thus, speaking is a challenge and a struggle for racialised students. Being conscious of our racialised location also affects how we participate in class. For instance, in attempts to escape labelling and being constituted as an angry 'woman of colour' or 'a passive Asian woman', I acted in ways to avoid being 'read' as such. I believe my own silence is the culmination of my fear of being 'read' and perceived by classmates in negative terms. Whatever I did, whether silent or engaged, I felt paralysed and immobilized to the extent that I could not participate in class discussions.

'Astarte' uses the term 'dominate' to explain what compelled her to fall back on patterns of silence. In this case, students who speak often set the pattern for the remaining semester because they occupy speaking space as if the classroom indisputably belongs to them. 'Astarte' explains how this feels:

> There are people who are really dominating, that always do the talking and really outspoken. I just don't bother. Logically, I know that I have a valid viewpoint, it could you know, change people's minds but I can't bring myself to. Like afterwards, I always say to myself, you know, I could have said something to that or I felt the same way or I don't think that person should make that claim, but I just can't do it in class.

I feel like I'm dominated.

'Pinky' attributed her silence in the classroom partially to classroom dynamics, and to her own feelings of inadequacy:

> I want to contribute, but I am afraid of being scoffed at, I don't speak the way the dominant voices in the class speak, so I end up thinking that what I have to say isn't important enough.

'Murdoch' outlined self-doubt, intimidation and the fact that her opinions existed outside of the 'norm' as factors in her silence:

> For one, I didn't trust myself enough or feel confident in what I was saying. Even though it made sense to me, I could just state an opinion that sounded so different from the norm. I think also, that there is a tremendous amount of pressure in the class, being felt from the other students, to say the right thing. I mean that good and articulate opinions are valued over others. I think that people really feel a need to intimidate me in a way, partly because they thought that they were more with it, or more feminist or smarter than me.

'Santa Maria' was not concerned with silence to the extent that the other respondents were; in fact, she seemed to display more confidence in terms of her role in the classroom.[11] However, she commented on being silenced from time to time in the classroom:

> It is good to speak. Like in highschool, I didn't. It's not like I have never had the experience where I couldn't speak. I have been silenced before and I am still being silenced. It is sometimes that I have a boiling point. You cannot shut me up anymore, and if you try, I am going to cry.

The inability to speak in Women's Studies classrooms was by and large the most important dynamic for racialised students' experience in my research. These experiences indicate the magnitude with which silence bears on racialised students. We expressed dismay because we could not participate in the learning process, and we felt disempowered and marginalised because of this disengagement.

Silence, as a product of gender socialisation for young (white) women's inability to speak, has been widely examined in feminist discourse. However, I must make it clear that there are common experiences for racialised women which add further dimensions to our silences and silencings. For example, we may experience internalized racism; a lack of knowledge of self, culture and history; and/or an ambivalence about identity and cultural background. All of these are reflections of the unique experiences of racialised minority women.

However, it is also of critical importance to see the conditions under which we do speak – conditions which can complicate matters of speaking and silence even further.

Authenticity and Speaking – When, What, How, for Whom?

In classes where the majority of students are white, racialised students are often called upon to speak on behalf of a cultural group or to represent the minority experience. This expectation, whether intentional or not, can present a greater issue for Canadian-born racialised minorities, many of whom may not feel 'different'. For example, in one discussion group, my classmates assumed that I practised Buddhism, and I was located as 'far too different' than what I felt comfortable with. 'Astarte' expressed the same concern, stating that, "it even bugs me even more when they think it's their mission to make me rediscover my culture. I don't want to be a spokesperson of something I don't know much about."

When asked to speak for all people of colour, racialised students are not only forced to confront their own 'difference', but are also expected to disseminate a 'difference' in speech that encompasses all people of colour. As a result, we often feel pressure to articulate authentic stories to an audience that is hungry for exoticism and adventure. Because of this, we often contemplate the content of our speech – when to talk, about what, for whom and on whose behalf.

When we are expected to speak solely and authentically from a cultural, ethnic or 'racial' standpoint, what little choice do we have but to entirely disengage or to feel isolated and uncomfortable? If we participate, our voices are heard as 'teachers' or 'experts' on issues of 'race', and nothing else. 'Murdoch' expresses this as a major concern:

> In a class discussion, or small group talk I think that I was there to give them some sort of perspective, or even as a teacher. I was basically there to teach them something that they didn't know. And I was not comfortable with that.

Because the only alternative conceptual category to (white) 'woman' circulating in Women's Studies classrooms is 'woman of colour' or 'Third World woman', I was asked about my 'Japanese-ness' – that is, about what white students saw as the oppressed, tradition-bound Japanese woman – which not only renders Japan's imperial history invisible and insignificant, but also homogenises and essentialises the experiences of all non-white women. Further to this, there was little interest in exploring my 'Canadian-ness' – neither in terms of the contributions that my community has made to the greater Canadian story, nor in terms of the Canadian state's relation to me and my community.

Classmates and/or professors, whether with good intentions or not, attempt to engage racialised students as 'native informants' in class discussions by directly asking questions or through subtle glances to demonstrate at whom a particular question was aimed. 'Astarte' framed the subtlety of classmates wanting her to speak in this way:

> I think one student in the class said that she wanted to know from someone else's experience, a 'visible minority' from their experience what they thought. And so, everyone looked my way. Sometimes I also feel like, Am I missing something? Should I know something about my culture that these people want that I don't know? I don't get it. ...
>
> I remember feeling stupid because I couldn't really answer the questions about my experience the students were asking. I felt like it was something I of all people should know, and be able to talk about yet I still couldn't think of the right thing to say.

'Astarte's' use of the term 'right' is well-suited to describing the expectation she felt to present an 'authentic voice' to her classmates. 'Astarte' acknowledges the existence of a 'right'/'wrong' thing to say; having understood this, she often felt stupid or inadequate because she was only asked to speak about her 'difference', as opposed to about her 'Canadian-ness'.

Authority – Given a Platform to Speak

Many of us, as racialised students, feel challenged or obliged to speak because, most usually, we are accorded a space to speak about 'race' – unquestioned and unproblematically.[12] This pressure is often times initiated by classmates who hope to be enlightened through another perspective, and sometimes through professors whose intent is to facilitate participation in the classroom.

On the subject of how classes are managed, 'Ferris' referred to the immediate assumption made on the part of her classmates that white women should not challenge women of colour writers; authority is predetermined for women of colour on issues of 'race'. She situated herself as someone who critically evaluates all writing:

> There was definitely a stereotype of how brown and black women should think. For example, in one reading the authors were insulting white women for looking like Pillsbury dough. I said it was a racist comment. But the class of white students decided it was not. As one older woman with gray hair put it, "I am not threatened by what they say because I come from a privileged class."

This is a significant statement about how classroom conditions can dictate the 'right' and 'wrong' positions/statements for women of colour to take/make. By virtue of their 'colour', women of colour are assumed to espouse and/or practice the same politics as a collective.

This assumption not only renders the individual differences between women of colour invisible, but also underscores 'non-whiteness' as the ultimate explanation for any statements we make or positions we take. When 'Ferris' diverged from the confines of what white women assume the politics and experience of women of colour to be, she is challenged on the grounds that she was speaking 'out of character'.

'Santa Maria' recounts situations where racialised minority students were offered a platform to speak only on issues of 'race'; outside of that, she observed that these students were discouraged from speaking. The underlying assumption that, in certain cases, speaking space should be allotted to particular students demonstrates the classroom as a 'white space'. Space is given and tolerated; white students bear no responsibility to carry on the conversation, and racialised minority students are regarded as 'teachers' whose role is to educate white students on 'race' issues. The assumption that white students should not or can not speak about race means that issues around race and racism are taken up strictly by people of colour. 'Santa Maria' offers an example of this:

> When there is an issue that they think is ours, they give that to us, but they quiet us down outside of that issue.
>
> Okay, well, when it comes to racism, I think we are seen as the experts. And we are accorded this space, but when it's another topic, well, that's the thing, when it's another topic, very few people try to integrate the issue of racism, as if it's a separate issue.

'Murdoch' noticed how her position changed from class to class. For her, there was one class that was exceptional to her overall experience in Women's Studies in which issues of immigration, citizenship and nationality were addressed. She noted the position that she was given as a 'minority' woman. The professor in this case was more sensitive to class dynamics. Here are 'Murdoch's' discoveries:

> Because I think she [professor] was expecting me to either to first all agree with what she was saying, I think she was expecting me to teach the class as well to go on and go on and get passed all of it. Like talk about citizenship and nationality and immigration. And I totally agreed with her. But how do you take it to that level? How do you fill that expectation that she has? I felt that my position changed from class to class.

When confronted with the reality of an 'alternate' way of being, such as of being 'different', 'Murdoch's' response reveals how even this potentially empowering position can also be intimidating and destabilising. Yet, although 'Murdoch' found the professor's attempt to bring out her voice uncomfortable at times, she was able to recognize that her own voice, despite its 'difference', was valuable. In this particular class, 'Murdoch' was encouraged to express her opinions. The instructor, who was also a racialised woman, opened up a space for her to critically negotiate her 'Canadian-ness' and 'Indian-ness' through concepts such as citizenship, nationality, and immigration.

For me, it was a real challenge to raise issues around racism and immigration, particularly during group discussions in which group members continually discussed patriarchy and sexism in terms of 'housewife oppression'. I struggled to address how, in my culture, staying home with children is not looked down upon and, is certainly not considered as living under the most oppressive of conditions. I struggled to express how such practices could be seen as a reflection of Japanese values that centre children and family over individual rights – and not as an indication of a backward society. Having a racialised professor address and speak to issues of immigration, migrancy, 'Third World' women's organizing, and nationhood suggested to me that my experiences *did* fall under the feminist agenda. This experience confirmed that feminism is not limited to deliberations on 'patriarchy', 'sexism', and 'body image' – or at least, that discussions around these topics should not take place outside of analyses of 'race' and racism. Courses that placed our issues as primary and relevant were instrumental in validating these marginal experiences. Somehow it shifted me from 'outsider' to 'insider'.

Overall, then, 'difference' is expressed not only as a negative and challenging aspect of our Women's Studies experience, as racialised students, but also as a site of empowerment and resistance. 'Visibility', or a racialised sense of self, became a stance from which we developed a sense of pride in coming to a consciousness about our 'difference'. This is best expressed by 'Murdoch' who captures the complexities and contradictions of a racialised location that is simultaneously alienating and a powerful form of resistance and empowerment:

> Soon I realized that difference could also be a tool, a visible marker for positive contribution and self-awareness. I felt really, really proud. I was getting used to feeling angry, knowing my difference that makes me feel proud of who I am. I am different. I am different. I never lost that pride. Knowing in my head that this is what I am, it really made me feel more positive.

I hold similar feelings, as I work through the various questions around 'difference' that inform this essay, and as I discuss these issues with other racialised students. As I do so, I begin to understand that my experiences are not isolated incidents. We are not alone, and, together, our issues demonstrate the 'realness' of the interconnections between 'race', class, and gender. Furthermore, the desire to see myself reflected back was achieved and fulfilled through sharing experiences and stories with other women who held similar experiences and positionings. This, in and of itself, is a form of resistance and empowerment, for it was these women who became the mirror from which I began to *see* myself.

Notes

1. Adrienne Rich, *On Lies, Secrets, and Silence: Selected Prose 1966-1978 (*New York: Norton, 1979), 199.
2. I place 'difference' in quotations to signify how dominant white culture views people of colour as 'different' from them and this does not necessarily reflect how people of colour see themselves.
3. Roxanna Ng, "A Woman Out of Control: Deconstructing Sexism and Racism in the University," *Radical In<ter>ventions: Identity, Politics and Difference/s in Educational Praxis*, eds. S. deCastell & M. Bryson (Albany State:University of New York Press,1989), 46.
4. Himani Bannerji, "But Who Speaks for Us? Experience and Agency in Conventional Feminist Paradigms," *Unsettling Relations: The University as a Site of Feminist Struggle*, ed. Himani Bannerji et. al (Toronto: Women's Press, 1991), 67-107.
5. Women's Studies should not be regarded as either monolithic or standardized. It is a complex set of structures and practices where not one overarching concrete ideology, discourse or pedagogy dominates.
6. This paper is based on my Women's Studies graduating research project, which was conducted at the University of Victoria, under the supervision of Dr. Jo-Anne Lee. In this research study, five racialised minority women participated in lengthy audio-taped interviews which lasted from one to three hours. Participants varied in age from early to late twenties. Participants were asked to provide pseudonym names for anonymity. The code- names that were given were 'Astarte', 'Murdoch', 'Ferris', 'Pinky' and 'Santa Maria'.
7. Trinh. T. Minh-ha, *Woman, Native, Other: Writing Postcoloniality and Feminism* (Bloomington and Indianapolis: Indiana University Press, 1989).
8. I can only offer partial accounts of racialised minority women's experiences in Women's Studies, drawing on a limited review of the literature, the experiences of a small number of participants and my own personal reflections. Thus, this paper is an analysis of a 'moment' in Women's Studies that is encapsulated in time and space and accessible through the lens of experience.
9. bell hooks, *Talking Back: Thinking Feminist, Thinking Black* (Boston MA: South End Press, 1989), 160.
10. In exploring the experiences of racialised minority women students in Women's Studies, it is important to maintain that there is no 'true' racialised minority woman's experience that can be generalized to all racialised minority students. We differ in terms of experiences, ethnicities, histories, class, and understandings of self.
11. "Santa Maria" immigrated to Canada as a teenager having experienced what it is like to be part of a majority.
12. In some instances, a platform was generally made available by fellow students, hoping to explore other experiences described in texts. In other words, putting a face to a theory or narrative brought forth in a text is reason enough for asking a racialised student to articulate her experience as a minority; students become tangible objects in relation to texts.

Selected Poems

Wil George

Writing Off the Indians

(a found poem from *The Imaginary Indian* By Daniel Francis)

Canadians did not expect Indians
to adapt to the modern world.
Their only hope was to assimilate,
to become white,
to cease to be Indians.
Any Indian was by definition
a traditional Indian,
a relic of the past.
The only image of the Indian presented
was a historical one.
The image can not be modernized.
Indians are defined in relation to the past
and in contradistinction to White society.
To the degree they change,
they are perceived to become less Indian.

Raven Flight

beak by precious salmon flavoured beak
wing by majestic wing to wing wingspan
I rise and fall
fall and rise in the rain
ocean salt wind caresses my flight
in the twenty first century
I have a right to fly
I have a right to land in a cedar tree
I have a right to perch myself there
peaceful inspiring breath
and painful mournful breath
catch salmon
feed pieces
piece by piece
asking praying knowing
that I am one part of a whole
ocean I plunge
beak talon on salmon
caw
beak by sweet black-berry covered beak
wing by strong determined wingspan

Raven's Take On Colonization

she flies as high as she can
she flies as fast as she can
with strength and determination
Raven flies

oh press   oppression
oh press your will your desires
your values and beliefs
upon those of others

impression   Raven is not impressed
with wind blowing amongst the people
that wind slicing through skin and bone
colonization is like a wind

sleek black wings and sharp precise beak
Raven says that wind like other winds
she can fly through   with some difficulty
but with strength and determination do fly through.

Raven Literature

One day, along the river bank,
I sit and read Norton's Introduction to Poetry.
As I'm engrossed in my reading,
Raven approaches unnoticed.
He raises his wings in greeting and
before he can get comfortable,
I engage him in conversation about my fascination
with English Literature.
I lecture on form, content, structure,
rhythm and metre.

Raven and I converse
over jarred salmon.
He says, "we goes halfers"
as I feast on those great poems
by Browning, Yeats, and Donne,
he feasts on the salmon,
oolican grease,
acquired taste
those pomes.

In between bites,
Raven tells me,
"poetry is story and people
have been storytelling for centuries
indigenous creative expressions
are story song and poetry
the people's connection to daily living
their connection to survival"

After lunch with Raven,
I realize that he is set in his way.
Unimpressed,
while I try to share with him
the virtues of English Literature,
the passion
of literary structure.

"no" he shakes his wings.
Raven says, "poem is a place
Go there sometime"

Not the Master's Tools:

Forms by People of Color

Tara Betts

Survival is not an academic skill. It is learning how to stand alone, unpopular and sometimes reviled, and how to make common cause with those others identified as outside the structures in order to define and seek a world in which we can all flourish. It is learning how to take our differences and make them strengths. For the master's tools will never dismantle the master's house. They may allow us to temporarily beat him at his own game, but they will never enable us to bring about genuine change.

– Audre Lorde[1]

The inception of a Third World Poetics class began in a writer's car where the two writers talking inside were seemingly on a path to nowhere in particular, particularly because Toni Asante Lightfoot and I were parked in front of my old apartment discussing how 'we' never have a place in the canon. How do we talk to young people who are not in the academy but in high schools, alternative schools, jails, community centers and churches and all the other places where African people often reside and congregate? These same people are rarely acknowledged as having experiences that are valid and credible enough fodder for poetry or much else in the world.

I asked myself what are the main criteria for a literary canon that can be taught beyond the characteristics of dead, white, male, that at one time, made me turn away from anything labeled classic, British, European? One of those criteria was the recognition and manipulation of poetic forms, especially English and European forms. The sonnet is no exception. When reading the thoughts about language from Jerome Rothenberg, June Jordan and Audre Lorde, I knew then that many people did not relate to forms that did not rise out of their own experiences. This is not to say that writers of the Diaspora have failed to acclimatize to the literary environments that compel them to follow established traditions—English, European or otherwise. We need only look at work by poets such as Marilyn Nelson, Lenard D. Moore, Dolores Kendrick or Gwendolyn Brooks to see how Black writers have utilized form as a tool to put forth images and histories that reflect the beauties and tragedies within Black communities.

I began to consider not only the transformation of European and English forms in Black hands, but how do Black poets and poets of color from other cultures nurture and sometimes revive the forms our ancestors created? How do we connect our present day language to traditions buried and still largely overlooked?

These inquiries resulted in the privilege to explore these forms as curriculum with high school students. As a creative writing teacher for several years, the idea of poetic forms by people of color did not even occur to me until I read on W. S. Merwin teaching Bantu combinations to some of his workshop participants. He was reading Jerome Rothenberg's *Technicians of the Sacred* during this particular workshop. Coincidentally, I then began to ask myself about how writers of color can write in form and still subvert a form like a sonnet or sestina to speak about resistance, struggle, and triumph.

However, these contemplations led me to explore the practical applications of poetic forms by people of color in the classroom. June Jordan's *Poetry for the People* emerged again in my pedagogical goals because she dedicated an entire chapter of this book to urging students to create their own canon.

In *Poetry for the People*, the students are looking at work with concern that includes all of humanity in literature. I also considered what are the norms that often disqualify writers of color as inferior to their white predecessors and counterparts.

One of those norms or expectations for writers is the ability and choice to appropriate form as a tool to create one's poetry. In short, how can the descendants of the dead white fathers take writers of color seriously when they do not know what a sonnet is, have not read one nor written one? Although this is a faulty line of reasoning when writers of color are often forced into double consciousness, as they must simultaneously study accepted masters and search for writers that reflect their cultural experiences. Studious, curious writers of color are often crammed into a predominantly white male tradition that Duriel Harris rebels against in "Villanelle for the Dead White Fathers." She proclaims "Don't need your blessed doctrine to tell me what to write and when." Harris continues to challenge classically-recognized forms such as the sonnet, triolet and the sestina with lines like the following:

> Shish kebab heroic couplets and serve 'em dipped in barbecue,/Slap-bass blank-verse-lines, tunin' fork tines 'til you think I'm Milton's kin./ Indeed, God made me funky. There ain't nothin' I cain't do.[2]

For Harris to choose the villanelle and utilize the repetition of blues-inspired vernacular implies an understanding of a form that was not created in an environment that believed she would comprehend and manipulate language, much less poetic form. She concludes with "there ain't nan thing I cain't do." She can use the often-studied forms and use the tongues of her Southern, blues-drenched predecessors at the same time.

Carol E. Miller makes note of how a widely accepted form can challenge what is inflicted upon students as the excluding standard in writing by briefly discussing the defiant sonnet "If We Must Die" by Claude McKay:

> McKay appropriates the form to contest its power, its authority as a

> part of a tradition that has excluded and silenced him, and to empower himself. Like Caliban, McKay has learned to curse in poetry that poses a direct challenge to both the oppressor's superiority and the way he has used poetry to oppress.[3]

A forced double consciousness about the canon, such as that displayed in McKay's sonnet and Harris' villanelle, led to extremely valuable questions. What are the forms that our people have created? What are the discernible patterns of African, Asian and Latin American writers? How did the writers of the First Nations capture their thoughts in recognizable beats? Have we not established our own sense of meter, literary devices as well as our own lexicons to share our experiences?

To begin teaching forms by people of color challenges the notion that the literary canon can only consist of English and European forms, which are often upheld as the standard. The high school students were oblivious to this consideration, but they began posing questions as we read about the Cuban son derived from Bantu people brought to the island's shore and its parallels with the African-American blues form. We explored why it was so difficult to find forms by African and Native American cultures and how performance-related forms are still poetic forms because there are poetic conventions and patterns that are readily identifiable in the work. We even talked about how translation can be a powerful tool in reinterpreting a poem to reflect the translator's politics, which may remind some of a line from Adrienne Rich's "The Burning of Paper Instead of Children." Rich reminds us throughout the poem, "this is the oppressor's language yet I need it to talk to you."[4] These are politically-charged concepts that question the purpose and power of poetic form in the hands of marginalized writers.

These conversations were easily developed among the class in both 10-week sessions since the non-profit organization Young Chicago Authors, which is influenced by the cultural relevance of June Jordan's approach, the liberatory pedagogy of Paulo Friere and project-based learning around publication and performance. There are difficulties in adapting to this approach for educators who are used to traditional ways of communicating where the teacher acts as an authority more than a facilitator and resource, but it seems to be a natural method of building relationships and inquiring about participants' interests as they pertain to a given topic. This approach accommodates their lives and concerns as a multicultural group that is curious about how people interact with each other in a diverse environment. These discussions mirror some of the thoughts in bell hooks' Teaching to Transgress:

> Accepting the decentering of the West globally, embracing multiculturalism, compels educators to focus on the issue of voice. Who speaks? Who listens? And why? Caring about whether all students fulfill their responsibility to contribute to learning in the classroom is not a common approach in what Friere has called the "banking system of education" where students are regarded as passive

> consumers. Since so many professors teach from that standpoint, it is difficult to create the kind of learning community that can fully embrace multiculturalism.[5]

In this instance, both sessions of the course were taught to not only include writers of color as active participants in establishing forms that are parallel to similar European forms and sometimes predate these forms, but to compel students to ask about their location in history. The majority of the students involved were young people of color. They were encouraged to write in their native tongues and translate if they chose to translate. Some of the students adapted slang in order to use the form in a more current fashion, and others were simply surprised to discover that poems emerged from the cultural communities that raised them.

One discussion revolved around the lack of Latin American forms. The decima, for example, is not one of the forms that Stephen Tapscott mentions in his anthology Twentieth Century Latin American Poetry. Tapscott's collection, although comprehensive, points out throughout his introduction that Latin American poets are heavily influenced by European traditions. Pat Mora discusses this form in her essay, "The Decima: The Poetic Journey from Spain to New Mexico," and the literary heritage of this form used by Sor Juana Ines de la Cruz. Although Spain is entrenched in its European roots, is this not a form rooted in the language of Spanish-speaking people that deserves to be noted? Apparently Mora thought so when she wrote her collection *Aunt Carmen's Book of Practical Saints*. The same can be said of Agha Shahid Ali's arduous work to promote the Arabic form of the ghazal before his death when so many people were loosely following the form. Both Shahid and Mora were seeking to write in the voices and the forms that spoke to the cultures within their skins and their homes. The situation of these writers living in the skins and homes that emerge from their publications is no different from the existences that Black writers have inked between lines, especially when considering their absence from the canon.

As we studied the various poetic forms used and developed by writers of colour, the students began to ask about the geography and landscapes and the time periods in which these forms existed. They wanted to know if a particular form connected to their distant family heritages, or if they could research their homeland's poetic forms. Some of them felt connected to the cultures that, prior to the experience, they only called themselves in name. For the sake of avoiding repetition, some of the student's comments will speak for them.

Luis Benavides, a 17-year-old senior of Mexican descent explained his connection with poetry and its spirit eloquently.

> I feel so connected to the past, my culture and the common culture of humanity and words. There is a common thread between the past

> and present in the spirit of expression and spiritual elevation through art. I've been inspired to write with that African, Korean and Native American voice, allowing myself to touch on those rich cultures and traditions of the world. Not all the forms were sonnets and sestinas nor should they be. Just like poetry has new frontiers and building blocks and stepping stones whether it's taught in English 101 or not.[6]

Cristina Correa, a young Puerto Rican woman, spoke succinctly. "Research is key and a feasible option in finding new poetic forms and their history." Another comment she made resonated with humor. "Privilege is annoying."[7] While soft-spoken, smiling William Swire admitted that he had learned more about his African and Jamaican culture. He was engaged by "the discussions about the African praise poems because it had to do with my heritage and I've never seen or read any types of poetic forms from Africa."[8]

In the midst of this table full of young writers, tooth sucking and/or eye-rolling could be guaranteed from David McLendon who compared the writing workshop to his creative writing class at the high school he attended where his teacher only taught them haiku, a Japanese form, but only one form nonetheless. His teacher who apparently was unaware that David was learning about all of haiku's cousins and its forerunner, T'ang poetry, a form often taught by June Jordan and discussed in her essay, "A Far Stretch Well Worth the Effort."[9] Would his teacher have been upset or assumed him disrespectful if he had begun to list somonka, renga, tanka, sedoka, haiga and haibun among other Japanese forms rooted in five and seven-syllable lines?

If writers of color continue to create their own traditions, as Sterling Brown and Langston Hughes did with the blues, as Afaa Michael Weaver has with the Bop poem (used by poets such as Lyrae Van Clief Stephanon among others), as Sonia Sanchez and Amiri Baraka respectively claim the sonku and the low coup, Black writers are building upon the foundations of the Dogon tige, the Cuban son, the eintou and many other African forms and making people ask what are the tools that African people used as architects of language? If writers of color consistently begin to consider the value of their formalist traditions and allow cultural experiences to expand notions about poetic form, then we begin to say that the canon is not as limited as some writers and critics would permit it to be.

As teachers who are striving to represent ourselves and our children in literature and history, we should expect questions, curiosity, indignation and excavation for inclusive realities with our faces, words and memories. So I envision David's twisted lip in my mind and I smile. Form, in this case, becomes a Bantu couplet, a two-line poem much like a haiku, where the first line represents something in nature and the second line is the object that is comparable to the image from nature in the preceding line. If our forms acted as a Bantu poem, it might sound like this:

Seeds burst into baobab and banyan trees.
Our forms grow thick, difficult to cut.

Notes

1. Audre Lorde, "The Master's Tools Will Never Dismantle the Master's House," in Sister Outsider (Freedom: The Crossing Press), 1984, 112.
2. Duriel Harris, *Drag* (Minneapolis: Elixir Press), 2003, 53.
3. Carol E. Miller, "The Other Harlem Renaissance," in *After New Formalism: Poets on Form, Narrative, And Tradition*, ed. Annie Finch (Ashland: Story Line Press), 1999. 52.
4. Adrienne Rich, "The Burning of Paper Instead of Children," in *The Will to Change: Poems 1968-1970* (New York: Norton), 1971.
5. bell hooks, *Teaching to Transgress: Education as the Practice of Freedom* (New York: Routledge), 1994, 40.
6. Luis Benavides, Personal interview, 2003.
7. Cristina Correa, Personal interview, 2003.
8. Willian Swire, Personal interview, 2003.
9. June Jordan, "A Far Stretch Well Worth the Effort," in *Some of Us Did Not Die* (New York: Basic/Civitas Books), 2002, 20-22.

Additional References

Ali, Agha Shahid, ed. *Ravishing Disunities: Real Ghazals in English*. Hanover: Wesleyan UP, 2000.

Gleason, Judith. *Leaf and Bone: African Praise-Poems*. New York: Penguin, 1994.

Guillien, Nicolas. *Patria o Muerte!: The Great Zoo and Other Poems*. New York: Monthly Review Press, 1972.

Jordan, June. *June Jordan's Poetry for the People.*

Mora, Pat. "The Decima: The Poetic Journey from Spain to New Mexico." *An Exaltation of Forms: Contemporary Poets Celebrate the Diversity of Their Art.* Ed. By Annie Finch. Ann Arbor: University of Michigan Press, 2002.

Rothenberg, Jerome, ed. *Technicians of the Sacred: A Range of Poetries from Africa, America, Asia, Europe & Oceania*. 2nd ed. Berkeley: University of California Press, 1985.

Skelton, Robin. *The Shapes of Our Singing: A Comprehensive Guide to Verse Forms and Metres from Around the World*. Spokane: Eastern Washington UP, 2002.

Turco, Lewis. *The Book of Forms: A Handbook of Poetics*. 3rd ed. Hanover: UP of New England, 2000.

Transgressive Voice:

From Where Do I Speak as a Black Woman?

Donyell L. Roseboro

Scanning the row of boys fidgeting across from me, I look desperately for a friendly face ... one who would choose me. Watching their eyes cast downward and stare with fixation at their shoes, I realize they are avoiding me. With a peculiar knot developing in my stomach, I sense that there is something more to their avoidance. I am not being ignored because I am ugly, smell bad, or talk too much. I am being avoided because I am the only black girl among the sea of potential dance partners awkwardly waiting to be chosen. This fact hangs clearly above my head, as if the teacher had written a sign saying, "Whites with Whites Only, Blacks with Blacks Only." By default, the only black boy in the room selects me as his dance partner, but does so with such contempt I begin to wonder if I am indeed ugly as well. I feel sorry for him because he had to choose me and sorry for me because I had to be chosen by him. For the first time in my seven years, I realize that my race distinguishes me from my gender. And it does so in a way that makes me feel alone. So I dance, with a partner who shares my skin color, but disparages me at every turn while I say nothing. I am completely silenced.

As I reflect on this memory as an adult, I face the realization that black women experience race and gender in ways that escape description while demanding explanation. Though I place the above experience on paper, its solidifying into words does not guarantee a complete understanding by the reader of the complexities of my feelings and thoughts. Yet it is precisely the personal (my experience of being silenced) that must be connected to the political (the larger structures which force such silencing). As an adolescent, I learned to speak two languages – one black yet reflective of the community in which I lived and one white yet reflective of the schools I attended. Most importantly, I struggled with learning when to speak and when to remain silent as a young black woman. As an adult, I now question the convergence of black and woman into a singular identity. Is my blackness merely an adjective to my femaleness? Or has my blackness, in its first place positioning, engulfed my woman-ness? Am I merely a chocolate covered XX? As I navigate a world which defines me before I can formulate a coherent identity, I am faced with one particular question: How do I speak *my-self*?

It is this personal struggle with voice that pushes me to analyze its development, confinement and liberation. In this effort to analyze the concept of voice as it relates to black women, I must develop at least a working definition of voice and black gendered consciousness. Considering the lengthy debates that have included voice, consciousness, race and gender as separate entities, I resist limiting these concepts to any singular definition and will attempt to define without categorically confining. With these linguistic challenges in mind, I structure this paper by first describing the concept of voice, relating it to gendered racial consciousness and providing final implications for black gendered voice to social agency. Ultimately, in analyzing voice as tri-dimensional, consisting of the inner, bridge and collective, I argue that black women's voices overcome muting through transgression – eruptive resistance against those structures and ideologies which dichotomize and polarize the self[1].

Important here to the concept of transgression are the distinctions between the self perceptions held by black women and the external perceptions held by those in power who maintain structures of domination. While black women were moving subtly to combat racism and sexism for centuries, those in power either ignored these expressions or tightened control to stifle them. As a consequence, transgression holds multiple meanings. For black women, I use it to describe the ways in which they abruptly and aggressively challenge patriarchy, sexism and racism. At the same time, I use transgression to describe the perspective of racist and sexist whites who responded to the black woman's voice only when it screamed in protest. In this way, transgression implicates a deliberate and personal move toward personal wholeness while simultaneously expanding existing external boundaries.

To understand this scream of protest and boundary shifting, Gayatri Spivak's essay on subaltern studies sheds additional insight into the idea of social change precipitated by a violent event. She says, "A functional change in a sign system is a violent event. Even when it is perceived as 'gradual,' or 'failed,' or yet 'reversing itself,' the change itself can only be operated by the force of a crisis."[2] I will draw on two concepts from Spivak's assessment to provide a foundation for our understanding of black women's voices as catalysts for social change. First, I am beginning with the assumption that black women, during slavery (whether they were slaves or not), existed as subaltern. Their voices, as individuals and the collective, could not surmount the entrenched institution of slavery and the social norms that regulated cross-racial relations, nor could they manipulate existing power structures to force a change in externally imposed gender identity. In essence, those in power refused to hear them because they were black and female.[3] Second, I am also beginning with the assumption that black women did and do protest, whether by voice or body, against racism and sexism in gradual ways. Our existence represents more than a continual string of crises aimed at dismantling the structures that silence us. Sometimes, we whisper protest. But because these whispers go unheard, social change appears as a violent event.[4] Hence, black women's voices force social change when they transgress – when they speak beyond established boundaries and disrupt the dominant social system.

Building on that theoretical framework, I suggest that voice manifests itself in multiple ways, that of the inner, bridge and collective.[5] The inner voice appears most often as an intuitive response – a way of knowing that resists clear explanation, but forces us to recognize its presence. It is, "the hallmark of women's emergent sense of self and sense of agency and control."[6] It positions itself as the 'I' in a given statement. In contrast, the collective voice incorporates that of the community. It implies a consciousness of self operating within a larger social context. According to Antonio Gramsci, consciousness in this sense suggests an "ideologically coherent ... spontaneous philosophy of the multitude."[7] Fundamentally, the collective voice speaks with a cognizance of the community (whether it be psychological or physical) and an understanding of separateness.

Between the inner and collective voice, I place the idea of voice as bridge. As such, it encompasses the myriad manifestations of voice somewhere between the inner and the collective. In this manner, the bridging voice connects the subject to its accepted community – that to which it chooses to belong. Although bridge voice connects, there is no definable starting and ending point. Inner voice does not necessarily preclude collective voice – they are contingent upon the other.[8] As individuals born into a larger whole, we inevitably create a self-consciousness defined by and against a collective consciousness. Each consciousness and its respective voice exist in relation to the other. It is these multiple and competing identities which mediate with which voice we speak and when.

Perhaps what makes this bridging voice most critical is its creation of transgressive space. Within the multiple bridges which connect converging personal and political identities, we attempt to relate the 'I' with the 'They'. It is in this space that we make decisions, analyze our own arguments, and decide to resist or to conform. It is an active space, one that requires kinesthetic connection between the private and the public. Here, we may choose between passivity or interjection. Because our identity is multiplicative,[9] we use this bridge space to bring unity to the multiple yet singularly coherent identities with which we live. This connected space gives birth to an 'I' who enters the public realm cognizant of her personal beliefs and willing to transgress boundaries which defy those fundamental presumptions of self.

Connecting voice to consciousness proves pivotal to our understanding of the expression of black collective identity. Once I establish a framework for black consciousness, I can later explain its relationship to gender and the formulation of black feminist perspectives. Considering the post structuralist notion of language as the shaper of identity, I begin with the descriptor, *black woman*. The juxtaposition of these two words affects the ways in which black women have been defined and define themselves. We are first black and then women. Race supersedes gender.[10] What then does it mean to be black? There are two theoretical foundations critical here to my exposition of blackness. First, I rely on Frantz Fanon's insistence on a distinctive black consciousnesses. He maintains:

> The dialectic that brings necessity into the foundation of my freedom drives me out of myself. It shatters my unreflected position. Still, in terms of consciousness, black consciousness is immanent in its own eyes. I am not the potentiality of something, I am wholly what I am. I do not have to look for the universal. No probability has any place inside me. My Negro consciousness does not hold itself out as a lack. It is. It is its own follower.[11]

While I do not suggest that there is a universal black consciousness perfectly replicated in each black individual, I do believe in a socio-historical notion of black consciousness bounded by the racialised experiences of black people in America and the collective spirit imbued in/on us as 'Other'. In this way, I lean towards W. E. B. Dubois' idea of "double consciousness."[12] As 'Other' in a white dominated society, black people have come to define themselves through the eyes of racist whites while simultaneously claiming a separate psychological space for self affirmation. In this way, Fanon and Dubois implicate a distinctive black consciousness capable of self-assertion or negation. Yet, to speak from a black consciousness that reflects a dual positioning in society (as either powerful or powerless) negates the multiple ways in which voice operates in conjunction with race. We are forced to consider voice as an incomplete representation of our multiplicative identity.

To then also refer to myself as a woman comes with inherent meanings imposed by history and the societal structures created within it. What it meant to be a black woman in the American south in the 1920s was different from what it meant to be a black woman in the north, or a white woman in either geographic locale. Race and gender intersect with time and location to yield a temporally charged consciousness bound by changing historical contexts. Contingent upon time, location, gender and race, voice seemingly suffers from an inability to provide coherence to existence — to speak so that others understand implies a necessity in bringing order to singular selves which negotiate an 'I'.

Considering the prevailing (if contested) ways in which black gendered voice is recognized in the political and social realms, I am plagued by several questions. What language does 'the black woman' speak? What does she say? What does she hear and interpret? To frame an answer by connecting the historical with the present, I return to the idea of muting and transgressive voice. Prior to the abolitionist movement of the 1830s, black women suffered in political silence. While their hopes and fears may have been recognized in the social realm and within the community in which they lived, these dreams and aspirations held no space in larger society. The institution of slavery and those who enforced it individually and collectively silenced them. How, then, does the black female slave come to voice and identify herself as woman?

She comes to this identity within a black consciousness existing in tandem with white collectivity. Though white men (and women) may have politically defined her as chattel, she was simultaneously treated as a gendered sex object/subject by white and black men. In this way, her body became a site of exploitation and resistance to the white oppressor while simultaneously serving as a site of love and respect to those welcomed into her presence.[13] By giving birth to and raising children, she ensured the survival of the race. When faced with the theft of her children, husband and body, her very survival created/reflected multiple identities specific to being black and female. Her survival indicates that she was never completely silenced.

From this perspective, the body becomes a metaphor for voice. Its existence and manipulation represents an identity that proclaims presence and, in its presence, speaks volumes. With her body, the slave woman who survived to see freedom proclaimed her-*self*. In freedom, she could then reflect upon her existence with a gendered racial consciousness and ponder the question of identity. According to DuBois, "As one of our black women writes: only the black woman can say 'where and when I enter, in the quiet, undisputed dignity of my womanhood, without violence and without suing or special patronage, then and there the whole Negro race enters with me." This consciousness would provide coherence to the seemingly competing identities of race and gender.[14] These historical implications continue to permeate current society which struggles with more covert forms of racism and sexism. To ultimately speak as a black woman, then, has profound ramifications on how we speak as black women and as a people today.

A post-structuralist framework suggests that "language speaks us" and, therefore, creates our meaning, as well as the myriad ways in which we voice these meanings. We can neither avoid language, nor avoid the social implications, suppositions or realism created by it. Gramsci viewed language as a "living thing and a museum of fossils of life and civilization."[15] As a preserver of history and creator of reality, language provides the stage and setting for gendered racial consciousness, as well as for feminism. In this way, it constrains as well as liberates through time and space. Depending on from when and where we speak, language becomes a tool for construction, destruction or deconstruction. Just as the slave woman complied by using the master's language, so she also resisted in code. According to Kathleen Casey who uses narratives of black women teachers in her research, "To be in the master's house is not necessarily to be under the master's control."[16] Though hegemonic, the master's control is never total; there is always space for manipulation and contestation. As a tool of domination and liberation, language thus stands as the greatest obstacle to and chisel for developing black women's voices.

Yet, language itself does not comprise the whole of black women's existence. We are *more than* language. Our physicality connects with discourse to create an embodied persona who acts beyond language.

As connected, the bodies and language reflect social and regulatory norms, as well as metaphysical and ontological relations. Butler explicates this point by saying:

> Here the body is not an independent materiality that is invested by power relations external to it, but it is that for which materialization and investiture are coextensive. Materiality designates a certain effect of power or, rather, is power in its formative or constitutive effects. Insofar as power operates successfully by constituting an object domain, a field of intelligibility, as a taken-for-granted ontology, its material effects are taken as material or primary givens. These material positives appear *outside* discourse and power, as its incontestable referents, its transcendental signifieds.[17]

Though Butler warns against accepting givens, and asks us to pay attention to the power relations involved in identifying those givens, her point regarding the materiality of the body is particularly relevant to this discussion. The body is power just as it creates, conforms, resists, questions and disrupts existing power relations. When its materiality changes, so does its contextualisation; when its contextualisations change, its materiality changes as well. As such, race and gender, as physical representations of the body, reconstitute our definitions of and reactions to intersecting relationships of power. For this reason, black women's bodies cannot be configured, defined, described, or discussed as equivalents to others because they are materially different, invested as they are with historically prescribed contextual assumptions. Materiality – though it sometimes escapes language or escapes being fully reduced to language – is shaped by it. In this way, the body defines and is defined by language. And herein lies the crux of the issue: black women, as historically, politically, and materially specific and distinct, create a discourse while simultaneously being created by it.

Voice Beyond Black Gendered Consciousness[18]

Transgressing the normative or regulatory discourses that constitute 'the black woman' also implies a recreating of identity within and beyond existing gendered and racial frameworks. We can thus reject stereotypical notions of ourselves as powerful black women, mammies or Jezebels and embrace alternative subjectivities. In this re-identification, we must also contend with competing claims on our expression. If we, at any time, refuse to speak 'as a black woman', we find ourselves summarily rejected by black communities and misunderstood by female counterparts. In doing so, however, we challenge Robin Morgan's notion that 'sisterhood is global' and instead enact Bernice Johnson Reagon's idea that sisterhood involves coalition building.[19] Race and gender do not guarantee psychological or physical connection.

To push this point further, I believe that we, as black women should be able to speak beyond being black and female, but should question the place from which we speak if we disregard or de-emphasize our gendered racial consciousness. Are we, to coin Hortense Spiller's phrase, then speaking "from nowhere at all?"[20] By implication, are we re-inscribing white racist and sexist notions of black women as objects rather than subjects? Are we denying our race and our gender? And finally, are we, in our refusal to give voice to a recognizable or intelligible black gendered identity, assuming the impossible? In a sense, is it possible to re-identify when one's identity relies so heavily upon the body, on that which is visible and already socially constructed?

Theoretically, I believe that accepting this power for re-identification is critical to the idea of black women as social agents. As a black woman, however, I find that any attempt to do so conflicts with my soul, makes me temporarily incoherent and forces me to create new space outside of existing language. Regardless of how this prescribed gendered racial identity came to be, I exist within, speak from and redefine it. In that sense, I am oppositional.[21] I define myself in relation to whatever is not me, while I also believe that I possess the power to re-define myself beyond what is currently explicable, definable, or linguistically acceptable. In connecting the private to the public, it is this oppositional identity that defines my voice and gives me the power of self-definition. And herein lies our hope for transformative social change – when identity as multiple and coherent need not be confined to the assumed, but embodies the unexpected.

Notes

1. Here I rely upon bell hooks', *Teaching to Transgress: Education as the Practice of Freedom* (New York: Routledge, 1994).
2. Gayatri Spivak, "Subaltern Studies," in *The Spivak Reader*, eds. Donna Landry and Gerald MacLean (New York: Routledge, 1995), 206.
3. I use the word 'woman' to describe the socially constructed female and the series of social norms and regulations which are culturally and socially re-inscribed as well as challenged by this gender construct.
4. Here, Spivak also uses Paul de Mann, *Blindness and Insight: Essays in the Rhetoric of Contemporary Criticism* (Minneapolis: University of Minnesota Press, 1983), 8. de Mann makes a distinction between gradual change and insurgency. In periods of non crises, he suggests that there are varied and numerous ways in which people challenge the social structures in place, but periods of crises force a more immediate change and uprising.
5. See Belinda Robnett, *How Long? How Long? African American Women Leaders in the Civil Rights Movement* (Oxford: Oxford Press, 2000) for a more detailed discussion of African-American women as bridge leaders during the Civil Rights Movement.
6. Ibid., 68.
7. As cited in Gayatri Spivak, "Subaltern Studies," in *The Spivak Reader*, eds. Donna Landry and Gerald MacLean (New York: Routledge), 214.
8. See Paulo Freire, *Pedagogy of the Oppressed* (New York: Continuum, 1970) for a discussion of human existence as relational. He posits that we define

ourselves in relation to others. Hence, there is no 'I' without a 'non I'. Applied here, there must be a collective voice for an inner voice to exist.

9. Adrien K. Wing, "Brief Reflections toward a Multiplicative Theory and Praxis of Being," in *Critical Race Feminism*, ed. A. K. Wing (New York: New York University, 1997). With multiplicative, Wing maintains that we have multiple yet singular identities which comprise the self and when multiplied, yield a singular self (ie … 1 X 1 X 1 X 1 X 1 X1 = 1).

10. Since the beginnings of the fight for equality during the ante-bellum era in America, black women have postponed the struggle for women's equality to contribute to a more unified front within the black community. Although suffragists like Sojourner Truth and Ida B. Wells recognized the need for women's civil rights, they supported black men in their quest for equality. As a result, black men in America gained the right to vote with the passage of the fifteenth amendment during the reconstruction era and began to participate in congressional positions decades before women gained the right to vote in 1920. This historical privileging of race over gender continues to have profound repercussions within the black feminist movement.

11. Frantz Fanon, *Black Skin, White Masks*, transl. C. L. Markmann (New York: Grove Press edition, 1991), 135.

12 W.E.B. Dubois, *The Souls of Black Folk* (NY: Fawcett World Library, 2003).

13 For a discussion of the body as it relates to voice and gender, see also, Hortense Spillers, "Mama's Baby, Papa's Maybe" in *Feminisms: an anthology of literary theory and criticism*, eds. R. R. Warhol and D.P. Herndl (New Brunswick: Rutgers UP, 1987), 384-405.

14 As cited in Cally Waite, "Dubois and the Invisible Talented Tenth," in *Feminist Engagements: Reading, Resisting, and Revisioning Male Theorists in Education and Cultural Studies*, ed. Kathleen Weiler (New York: Routledge, 2001), 41.

15 As cited in Jane Kenway, "Remembering and Regenerating Gramsci," in *Feminist Engagements: Reading, Resisting, and Revisioning Male Theorists in Education and Cultural Studies*, ed. Kathleen Weiler (New York: Routledge, 2001), 50.

16 Kathleen Casey, *I Answer with My Life: Life Histories of Women Teachers Working for Social Change* (New York: Routledge, 1993), 141. Here, Casey relies upon the research of Katerina Clark and Michael Holquist, Mikhail Bakhtin (Cambridge: Harvard University Press, 1984).

17 Judith Butler, *Bodies that Matter* (New York: Routledge, 1993), 34-35.

18 For purposes of brevity, I choose not to explicate womanist ideology within this paper. This is not to suggest it holds any less significance for understanding black women's voice; it may provide a more complex understanding of black women with particular emphasis on issues of marginalization and spirituality. I cannot do the discussion justice within the confines of this particular paper. For more on womanist ideology, see Alice Walker, I*n Search of Our Mothers' Gardens* (New York: Harcourt Brace Jovanovich, 1983).

19 As cited in Chandra Mohanty, *Feminism without Borders* (Durham: Duke University Press, 2003), 116-18.

20 Hortense Spillers, "Mama's Baby, Papa's Maybe: An American Grammar Book," in *Feminisms: An Anthology of Literary Theory and Criticism*, eds. Robyn Warhol and Diane Herndl (New Brunswick: Rutgers UP, 1987), 384-405.

21 See bell hooks, "The Oppositional Gaze: Black Female Spectators" in *The Feminism and Visual Culture Reader*, ed. A. Jones (New York: Routledge, 2003), 94-105, for an in depth analysis of black women's gaze as a socially transformative tool, affected by/indicative of her physical presence in society.

Blankets of Silence

Rubina Sidhu

I had always regarded my identity as one constant stabilizing factor, an entity that would remain the same throughout my life. I believed I was born and would eventually die with the same identity: Indo-Canadian Girl.

I never forcefully examined this identity, placed upon my skin by higher powers, by powers that are unnamed, uncoloured, and ironically, unidentifiable. I travelled through public school, naming my identity as ' Indo-Canadian', then saying 'Indian', and finally coming to terms with 'Punjabi'. I thought to myself and truly believed that, in these simple alterations, I was actively defying the institutionalized mechanisms of conventional identity politics, including the 'unchoices' that structure the politics of naming. But looking back, I feel that I never knew fully why it almost seemed creepy to hyphenate my identity. These acts of hyphenation constantly reminded me that I was only half Canadian—half of an identity from which I was conceived, born, educated and will probably die. It was a funny, uncomfortable feeling as I heard white students, from elementary school to the present-day, actively permit each other to be 'just Canadian', even though they, like me, are visitors on this land.

When I entered high school I began to contemplate this further, and ask why certain people were forced to hyphenate, explain and label, while white men, women and children continued to colonize the label of 'Canadian' for each other. In part, this joint effort, perhaps even solidarity, among white people is what perpetuates colonial hierarchies of race and status within the current political climate. The persistent racism that is embedded in all facets of society is a dominant factor in how marginalised identities come to be seen and named within a white supremacist society. For marginalised identities, the process of naming ourselves on our own terms is thus a process of battling the racisms that structure our lives. The ability to 'be' is the fantastical position of choice, a place where marginal persons would hope to have the choice in naming and unnaming ourselves. 'To be' allows the chance to breathe, to live, to be silent by choice. But, where would I find a place at home where identity was positioned by choice, and not by coercion? Where would I find the solitude just 'to be'?

I was told once that I would never want to be in the mainstream, because it sucks, and I should not think of ways of getting out of the margins, because that is where action happens, that is where change occurs. But, how would I know that the mainstream is not for me when I have never been there? Who is that person to tell me that?

She, another marginal person, comes from experiences far different than my own. How would she know that, for once, I am just tired of fighting, tired of justifying, tired of spelling out my name and tired of thinking twice about the way people e-nun-ci-ate ev-ery-thing for me. When she informed me that the mainstream was not the team of choice, when she told me that I would do anything to get out of that place, I thought of my location and ultimately I thought of my history.

History is the marker of my identity, and as I enter any classroom, history is silently waiting. I hear history when isolation hits the bone of my being.

She waits, breathes and speaks.

There has been a silent blanket in my household as my sisters and I have never really heard the stories of isolation, oppression and blatant racism that my parents lived through when they first arrived to Canada. We never really understood the tragedy and violence that they endured in their new home. Lately, as discussions revolve around the modern-day racism that we, their daughters, go through, my parents now recognize and adopt language and feelings for what has happened over the past thirty years. I know the basic history of my father's travels: he left his house at sixteen to receive an education outside of his small and rural village. He came to Canada as a young man and continually had to 'work off the guilt' of being a 'burden' on his aunt and uncle who had commissioned him over. To this day, he 'works off the guilt' by answering to their beck and call because, to him, they gave him the ticket out and the ability to live a life only dreamed of in his small village. Tears shed inside me as my dad, while washing the dishes, tells me of his experiences in finding a job when he arrived alone to a foreign country. I want him to continue but he loses the language to express the violence that has yet to subside. He always begins by stating that "you would not even imagine…." And he finishes by saying, "that is why your mother and I want all three of you to finish university…just get educated." After he finishes, he goes on as if it was nothing, as if what he said is in the past, as if he is unscarred.

I understand that they were protecting me and my sisters, keeping us in a bubble and trying to believe that because we were born in this country, and because we have a fancy degree hanging on the wall, these Western markers of status would provide us the ability to be equal citizens of this country. But the constant struggle to name my own identity, to gain acceptance, and to contextualise identity politics remains a solitary effort. The institution of higher education becomes a place where quick questions follow even quicker answers. Does knowledge and recognition of identity politics sit with my Bachelors of Arts? If it does, where and how do I exercise it? I sit, questioning this, realizing that my father's dream of what education can provide and my personal experience with the desire to rebel against the whiteness of the institution are distant yet close partners in the lived experience of marginal persons. We all speak of the same problem, but we cope with many distinct mechanisms: linking time lines past to our future and fearing that, no matter what, we are guilty in believing that the next generation will have its own problems.

I speak of this guilt that my father carries for a specific reason. Living in the same house, just a few doors down from his aunt and uncle, I see his constant struggle to receive acceptance from an unknown source: they are merely a symbol of a bigger system and use guilt as a power tool to remind their servants that we will never be equal. I carry this guilt and all its baggage as I set goals and time lines to become 'successful'. These goals become the stagnant weight on my shoulders as I work off guilt that my father is too old to work off. If you ask me right now what this guilt looks like, I wouldn't know how to explain, but I would begin at my identity politic. Knowing my history is where I would begin; writing this down is where I would begin.

Often times there is a hesitation in recording, or a hesitation in searching for the recorded histories of margins. The margins, where stories lie well beneath the surface of privilege and greed, is where my histories remain and begin. As people archive different histories, even certain sorts of marginal histories such as feminist history, there is an eerie acceptance of not having to represent or be accountable to attendant histories of race and colonization. When I see a large number of white students discuss research that is perceived to account for a radical take on history and its implications in recording, I soon realize that my history is still not substantial for their activist archeology. They acknowledge the places they miss, yet the extent of their acknowledgement remains there: said but unsaid. The lack of marginal history remains in the voices and hearts of the marginal activists. They, who are not tooled with the knowledge of the master, remain in the fields working to provide food on the table, remain unlearned in grammar and carry their history alongside their passports, baggage and shoes. Marginal history remains intact with the physical and is not separate from everyday history. My parents and their three daughters have history stamped on their foreheads because 'as hard as we try' we will never be unmarked from the violence and hate from being half Canadian.

The construction of history, personal and public, constantly forces a black/white dichotomy of experience versus theory. This binary of oppositions forces a sense of depleted identity, an identity that must choose its location for the sake of adhering to normative practices of identity politics. I never recognized that I had politics within my identity; I was never told I had politic.

In the context of such identity politics, what does it mean to unname, or to unidentify? Paradoxically, my own process of unnaming myself has come through a struggle of beginning to acknowledge my name, my history, my identity. I need to clarify that this process of unnaming which I am describing is a symbolic unnaming, but at the same time, it is a dynamic process where questions, theory, and experience play pivotal roles in reclaiming, acknowledging, learning and adopting identities that fit the purpose of my being in particular contexts. I walk with this question about names into places where I am often already positioned within certain frameworks of learning and knowing. Education from the margins, from my marginal position, goes far beyond the classroom; it goes into the corners of everything I do. This journey to unname is a choice, but learning from the margins and engaging institutional education is merely a lifeline. It is hard to explain this process on paper, because emotions override this constant journey to reach a place where I do not question my position based on my name, my colour, or any other marker of difference. The difference in me is the same difference that threads an envious needle of wanting to feel acceptance.

And I Am Finding A Narrative In Between

Naomi Horii

& I am finding a narrative in between

A Vision for the Future[1]

(Before I begin, a few small questions:
How do I write between the
official narratives of the academic
institution? How do I develop
my own unique voice and create
meaning in the teaching/learning
environment? How do I re-root/
route my creative abilities inside the
university setting? To what extent
are these questions tied up with issues
of racism and antiracist practice?
To what extent does my university
practice antiracism?)

"People are what make our university:
students, faculty, staff and alumni.
Our principal focus in the years
ahead must be on those people.
Our goal is to recruit and retain
a diverse group of exceptionally
talented students, faculty and staff
and support them in ways that allow
them to reach their highest potential.
Our commitment to diversity, equity,
quality and supportive environment
will be paramount."

(But I have to ask: *when* will this be
paramount? And when do I begin
telling you about racism, in between
the narratives of the institution?)

"Objectives for the future"

"To ensure the principles of fairness
and equity are incorporated into
all procedures and activities at the
University of Victoria."

(Incorporation. This is the story of my experience in a classroom. My professor asks me to read my creative writing piece to the class, before he interrupts me mid-sentence to say that he can't understand a word I am saying. The class is deafeningly silent. The assignment has to do with our own experiences of 9/11, and I am critical of the racist images that are being shown on the media. I point to the racist backlash that we, as people of colour, have been increasingly facing. After interrupting me, my professor begins to teach a new lecture from that point onward, using specific references to my mistakes. He learns my handwriting. He knows to remember, but not how to pronounce, my name for next time.)

"To ensure that outstanding students from diverse regions and backgrounds have the opportunity to attend the University of Victoria and that there are no hurdles to admission except academic and creative potential."

(No hurdles except the 'standards' by which students become outstanding, academic, creative. Standards. Who sets these standards? Whose standards are these? How do these standards conform to and reproduce Eurocentric ideas of knowledge, intelligence, and creativity? In my class, the professor asks a favoured student to read her 9/11 piece, once again, and praises her for her creative allusions to Yeats, Joyce, and Eliot. It is not mentioned that this piece upholds the standards of only the western literary canon, that it romanticises war, and perpetuates fears of the racial 'other' or 'uknown'. This piece gets an A for its supposed 'universal' appeal. I allude to the racially victimized in the aftermath. The un-named. I get a C minus, because, I am told, my writing is not 'objective' enough.)

"To recruit and retain a diverse group of faculty, of the highest national and international standards, in those areas where UVic chooses to develop its programs of scholarship in teaching, research, professional and creative work."

(A diverse group of faculty and scholarship in teaching? When I go to see my professor about my assignment, he asks me how long I have been speaking English. He convinces himself that it is my second language, and he cannot fathom how I got this far. His questions and attitude replay stereotypical ideas about people of colour - that we do not speak English, that we are uneducated, that we are 'foreign' and 'other', that we do not belong. My professor asks me to seek 'help', and I continue to work harder than others to justify my writings.)

"To provide a learning environment that builds the sense of community possible at a university where the majority of students come from outside the local region."

(And how does my university honour the peoples whose land and poverty it profits from? I question how the marginalised, or the colonised, can find themselves in stories and histories if there is no existential safe place or space in which to do so.)

(My narrative must squeeze between the shapes that the institution dictates. It must fit into spaces of unreading, unhearing, unravelling. It must work to build coalitions beside/behind/underneath that of the official narratives here. It must take shape, form, and space.)

Notes

1. *A Vision for the Future*, from the University of Victoria's official website. All quotations, hereafter, are taken from this document. Available at http://web.uvic.ca/strategicplan/people.html.

Finding Narrative II

Naomi Horii

Studies in Education lead students toward an understanding of the nature of knowledge, its interpretation and how it is shared. Through individual and group work, instruction, and supervised experiences in the field, students in the Faculty develop their professional knowledge skills as well as their ability to share their knowledge and experience. In this way, students learn how to be leaders not only in the classroom but in the community as well.

– *University of Victoria Calendar online. Available at: http://web.uvic.ca/calendar2004/FACS/FoEd/index.html*

views from vancouver 2000-2003

the multiple views of place and space conflated is this painting of move
ment and travel, packing and unpacking, breaking down and reforming with time always passing,
aging, fording the connections, looking for borders and new views is this painting,
waking up every morning and still not seeing: newness is never necessarily about beginning

jennie duguay

when i speak can you hear echoes?

views from here

jennie duguay

1.

To speak ... means above all to assume a culture, to support the weight of a civilization.

– Frantz Fanon[1]

how

to speak
the assumptions i inhabit my perpetual desire to maintain opposition

to speak
from a consciousness echoing exclusions i'm filling in like tripping on
the weight of the histories my living's been living on

to speak
the language this mouth speaks staggering beside itself enclosed
speech so particular now i hardly want to support it

to speak
against my speech in my speaking?

2.

Even if we think we are not personally racist or sexist, we are clearly marked by the burdens and privileges of our histories and locations.

– Chandra Talpade Mohanty[2]

As the daughter of a middle class, french canadian, christian family of three i feel i have been, in general, raised and educated to conform to the standards set by the dominant settler (colonizing) culture in this country. I am now learning how these standards are constructed, in part, on a platform of assumed white normativity and superiority which provides benefits and privileges for whites. How has my history and location 'marked' me? What are the implications of these marks for my struggle against abusing the power of privilege? If i can access these marks, is transformation and healing a possibility? In some ways, it seems that my racialisation has determined how i have been raised and educated in the context of a white supremacist society – the power and legibility of which is thoroughly dependent on the systematic denial of racist and sexist histories of territorial, economic, educational, physical, and mental imperialism.

Western pedagogical practices are embedded in and with these denials, and thereby reproduce and encourage racism, sexism, heterosexism, elitism, ableism, and other forms of discrimination in both direct and indirect ways. These patterns have implications throughout the educational system and beyond. I believe that other students who can identify in one way or another with my background and/or my thinking may also identify with, and challenge, these beginning thoughts on and about the education that students – particularly students from socially dominant groups – are receiving. I began this paper after becoming angry and disappointed about the many stories and voices that my education has lacked, ignored, misrepresented, and suppressed. I had so many blank pages and canvases, so much air in between me and some sort of ground, some sort of connection to all the questions and thoughts about what western pedagogies are educating students towards. I wrote this paper because i want to learn and talk about "the West and its others so that education becomes the practice of liberation."[3]

3.

Education is a system of imposed ignorance.

– Noam Chomsky[4]

I've spent 18 of my 22 years in the canadian educational system and over three of those years in university studying english. For a variety of reasons, I decided to drop out of school this spring and get a full-time job. I had become very seriously disappointed and angry with the amount of time, energy, stress, and money i was spending on an education that i have come to believe can impose colonizing mentalities on students. I now understand this imposition as an action and an effect of a colonial educational system which is organised through patriarchal and white supremacist ideologies.

Every imposition can be repelled and resisted, though the shape, scope, urgency and impact of our resistances will vary and shift from one social context to another. I acknowledge that students experience and respond to colonial education in a variety of ways, and an important question seems to be: what is at stake, and for whom? In my case, and based on my personal experiences in school, I guess I'm worried. I'm wondering about and looking at what/how i've been taught, and what/how i've learned over the years, as well as the ways in which my instruction and learning have been influenced and informed by my social positionings. I'm interested in how western pedagogies can operate to obstruct students from challenging exclusionary education. By what means and in which ways might western educational institutions be preventing "education [from becoming] the practice of liberation?"[5]

4.

...[it is necessary] to think relationally about questions of power, equality, and justice, the need to be inclusive in our thinking, and the necessity of our thinking and organizing being contextual, deeply rooted in questions of history and experience.

– Chandra Talpade Mohanty[6]

Over the last three years, i've immersed myself fully in my education, studying western canonic literature and writing essays on topics from Beowulf to Chaucer to Cohen. In my courses and in my essays, i've at times found myself struggling to open up doors that have been deemed irrelevant, trivial, or non-existent (usually by those who occupy positions of privilege in this society) – spaces which, nonetheless, i know are there. The literature i've studied has most often been taught in ways which either ignore these doors or construct them as 'other', and as therefore unconnected to the study of english literature. "But what does colonization have to do with how we read Restoration literature today?" asked a confused second year UVic english professor after i questioned why this topic hadn't been addressed in class. At the time, i was unable to communicate to him that western cultural supremacy, patriarchy and other oppressive systems and ideologies are deeply woven into western literature and theory. I had neither the language nor the room to say this in my courses – space was not being made for students to analyse and critique the production and maintenance of western hegemony through its cultural products. I didn't understand then that the connection between the institution of western education and hegemonic power is one of mutual dependence.

The word 'hegemony' is one that i find challenging to understand and define. Hegemony is the power of domination, but is by no means static, discrete, or one dimensional. It is a state in which those in power may reference themselves, their experiences and their history as 'normal', and as the referent by which all 'other' experiences and histories are (mis)understood, measured and judged. Hegemonic power, while always in a state of more or less contestation and change, always involves a degree of consent on the part of a given populous. Recreated and maintained through educational institutions, the legal system, government, the media, and a variety of less formal systems of civil organisation and regulation, hegemony depends on the absorption of dominant ideology into the cultural common sense. To be sustained, hegemony requires the general complicity of current and future generations, and, in the west, the educational system seems significantly invested in this task of teaching towards the inheritance of generational ignorances.

In general, it seems that western pedagogies prefer to teach reading and understanding literature as if the only history relevant to these practices, and to the production of literature itself, is that of the west. This is one example of how histories of colonisation and western imperialism reflect through and inform cultural production and ideology. I'm trying to say that how literature is taught and read can hide and reveal a lot. If western educational systems were to recognize and address their relationship with western imperialism, would the West's hegemonic power shift dramatically?

Through these thoughts and questions, I am trying to acknowledge and express the multiple ways my upbringing and education have attempted to situate me outside of certain doors – as prepared to defend their non-existence or irrelevance. I must also take responsibility for my own refusals and struggles in order to make movement go and grow. I don't want to turn my back and take up the place my family and ancestors (however un/knowingly and to whatever varying degrees) have taken up. I am beginning to think about my experiences of how western pedagogies can produce courses and classrooms in which issues around colonialism and imperialism are rarely contextualised by professors, addressed in course texts, or questioned by students. I am beginning to imagine ways to open the doors which lead to the questions and movements which can fundamentally change the western educational system and its pedagogies. I am beginning to imagine an education which provides students with the space and the tools to approach these doors, open them, and be opened to them and by them. Beyond this imagining, i feel lost. Lost because i cannot see past the opening to the movements made by it, nor to the changes it could facilitate on personal and collective levels. Yet 'lost' is a space as well, and within it i will continue to imagine and wander around, hands grabbing and embracing openness.

5.

...ideas, cultures and histories cannot seriously be understood or studied without their force, or more precisely their configurations of power, also being studied.

– Edward Said[7]

In many ways, the study of literature is the study of ideas, cultures, and histories, yet studying systems of power and resistance, with the exception of women's studies and post colonial studies, doesn't seem to be considered useful or important by the western educational system. Perhaps western pedagogies will not recognize that "configurations of power" influence and inform the study of english literature, precisely because this recognition can trigger the shaking and cracking of the foundations upon and within which western hegemony operates. For instance, if, in a first year lit class, the professor were to encourage discussion around how notions of western/white supremacy are encoded into non/fiction, prose, etc.– into ideology – would students be more likely to question and consider imperialism and racism on historical, personal, local, national, and global levels? How would these sorts of discussions function to challenge hegemonic power within the institution and the English department? In my experience, many professors deny colonialism and racism by their neglect to consider it. Is denial a way of protecting the white imperial history celebrated by many canonized authors? Is denial also a way to avoid those feelings of discomfort which arise when white students are asked to talk about racism and colonialism? Disregarding histories of imperialism and the (white) male supremacy which fuels it results, among other things, in the propagation of racist and sexist productions of knowledge and representations of the 'other'. Disregard then, along with racism and sexism, are necessary to the functioning of western hegemony.

Since i hope to commit myself to counter-hegemonic consciousness and the production of anti-oppressive art and literature, i want an education that facilitates and encourages my understanding, development, and criticism of these questions and thoughts. I want to talk about how, in the study of english literature, standards of white cultural normativity are maintained by ignoring how western pedagogy privileges white imperial histories and experiences, while excluding and/or dismissing the histories and experiences of those whom it exploits and of those who resist oppression.

In some of my experience at university, exclusionary ways of knowing have been supported by the unwillingness and/or ignorance of professors whose incomplete lectures, course materials, assignments, and insistence on objectivity can prevent many students from seriously examining the imperial history and foundations of the literature they study (as well as their place within this history). How do these pedagogical practices work to prevent students, specifically those students who may, like myself, be looking at 'whiteness' for the first time, from actively deconstructing white privilege while participating in courses which actively reconstruct it?

6.

...the social ontology of both the writer and the reader (their social being in historical and personal times) not only shapes their intellectual/political views but also provides the necessary ground for a social and critically active form of reading.

– Himani Bannerji[8]

I have never really understood or believed in the insistence on and practice of objectivity. How can who i am not influence how i write about what i write about? How can understanding ever happen outside of who i am or without me? This is not only impossible, but totally ridiculous. Is objectivity a tool historically used by institutions and those in power to prevent threatening counter-hegemonic knowledges and truths formed in subjective experience from entering into the institution and creating change? If so, the fiction of objective thinking and learning are necessary to the maintenance and reproduction of western hegemony.

Devaluing subjectivity is one way in which western pedagogical practices encourage students to disassociate their selves (in all their social positionings) from their learning, understanding, and analysis. For example, students in Western institutions are generally required to reflect on, comprehend, and write about topics in philosophy, literature, psychology, law, etc., as if their own 'I' does not influence their 'take' on the issues being studied. Indeed, Western institutions of learning typically demand that the 'I' be removed altogether from student academic essays because of the so-called irrelevance of subjectivity. This denial of personal involvement and responsibility is, in part, a most necessary root of a 'healthy' imperial power – which is itself dependent on the silencing of counter-hegemonic knowledges and truths. For, if power acknowledges its power (its 'I' or 'I's'), by consciously locating its privileged self, it ends up sawing at its own arm. If students believe that self-positioning and self-criticism – their "social ontology"– is unnecessary, and even wrong, will there be any space for examining questions of power and privilege? How can practices of accountability and self-reflexivity be fostered in an environment where students are encouraged to understand themselves as neutral within, or abstracted from, the learning process?

In order for white cultural superiority to be normalised, and assumed to be universal and objective, it must be constructed again and again as such by western pedagogy. The invisibility of this referent allows certain students, under the guise of objectivity/neutrality, to produce 'Truth' – to learn, understand and communicate knowledge from the 'universal' perspective of the socially dominant group. Do the knowledges produced by those who accept standards of western (white) superiority work in the service of western hegemony and consequently contribute to racist and sexist pedagogies?

7.

...we share a commitment to language and to the power of language, and to the reclaiming of that language which has been made to work against us.[9]

– Audre Lorde

from where i be
here
holding tightly on

to openings i am convinced of
the only reason to keep on
moving and turning
want around the language i'm wanting
things i have to start and yet even so
this speaks to the whole of closed-up
thinking we can grow into knowing and i'm trying to
separate my whole self from
the temptation is always so teasing me
just to let go and who cares and how can i
can't i know no i wont say it
doesn't matter and see
these movements?
these movements i am making
medals of western training into scars i scratch
at what created belonging and longing to unlearn my longing for medals
myths of immobility alarms stinging my tongue when i ask for proof

8.

Overcom[ing] years of notions of what is normative...is about coming to believe in the possibility of a variety of experiences, a variety of ways of understanding the world, a variety of frameworks of operation, without imposing consciously or unconsciously a notion of the norm.

– Elsa Barkley Brown[10]

From where i be, this quote speaks to the essential processes of unlearning privilege and working towards solidarity with those historically subordinated, and to struggle both individually and collectively against modern imperial global capitalism which continues to oppress and exploit those who resist its domination. A part of this work requires that i continue to question and challenge the variety of ways i have been taught to assume western (white) normativity. These notes on beginnings are my some of my first efforts to put to language some of the layers and interconnections, the "variety of experiences" upon which i see norms and assumptions forcing themselves as the truth. I believe that neither the power and privilege invested in the colour of my skin, nor the imperial history of my culture is something i can simply 'unpack' or get rid of by following some guidelines in a book on allyship. Do i believe i can always be unlearning by accepting my privileges against themselves? Can i use privilege to fight for social justice? Although it seems to me that this work is intensely personal, i also feel that it must be done collectively. So how do people raised and educated to inhabit colonizing mentalities "surrender the power to act as colonisers?"11 Perhaps i might first ask "how do colonisers act?" and "how are these actions taught?"

9.

do we [those of us who would participate in the formation of counter-hegemonic cultural practice] position ourselves on the side of colonizing mentality?

– bell hooks[12]

My first reaction to hooks' question: "of course not! if we participate in counter-hegemonic practices it is impossible for us to be on the side of the colonizing mentality." On third or fourth thought, i have begun to think that hooks is, in part, pointing to what Chandra Mohanty addresses throughout *Feminism Without Borders*: the colonizing tendency of western feminists to uncritically assume white normativity and to place the western woman as the standard by which "third world" women are then defined, evaluated, and othered. In this case, i feel like it takes much more than simply defining myself as an anti-racist, anti-capitalist feminist to actually work for and towards decolonisation. What does it take? For now, i think it might involve acknowledging the power of recognition as a trigger of personal impetus for change; consistent positioning and repositioning of my self within "configurations of power"[13]; attempting to steep my consciousness and living in counter-hegemonic resistance; and realizing that the actions i take part in and make are themselves part of a global movement of resistance which has been moving and growing since the beginning of oppression. I'm hoping that my beginnings, questions, and thoughts on and against hegemonic western pedagogies as i feel i've been taught and experienced them at this point in my life can provide points of discussion, reflection, objection, criticism and specifically (hopefully) varieties of personal and organized resistances from students within the institution. I want to challenge myself and others to create communities of resistance within the university in order to affect personal, collective, and institutional changes in western pedagogical practices. These notes have been a place of beginnings and movements for me. I know that they will grow and change as i do, and i welcome and look forward to opening up with your responses.

10.

Resistance lies in self-conscious engagement with dominant, normative discourses and representations and in the active creation of oppositional analytic categories.

– Chandra Talpade Mohanty[14]

for the past two years or so i've been collecting
these strings   so to speak
scattering and recollecting strings thru out
my pockets and drawers and spaces
i've begun to recognize patterns and places

where what seemed contradictory or parallel
overlaps
these questions have begun to formulate
answers in the forms of feelings
opening me up to a place where i can begin
to speak the feelings and ask the questions
i see now i've taken the opportunity to begin
braiding this always expanding string
collection into what i can only believe
is becoming a weapon

Notes

1. Frantz Fanon, *Black Skin White Masks* (New York: Grove P, 1967), 17-18.
2. Chandra Mohanty, *Feminism Without Borders: Decolonizing Theory* (Durham: Duke UP, 2003), 191.
3. Mohanty, *Feminism Without Borders*, 200.
4. Noam Chomsky as cited in *Manufacturing Consent - Noam Chomsky and the Media* [videorecording], dir. Mark Achbar and Peter Wintonick, 1993.
5. Mohanty, *Feminism Without Borders*, 200.
6. Mohanty, *Feminism Without Borders*, 192.
7. Edward Said. "Orientalism," in *Colonial Discourse and Post-Colonial Theory: A Reader*, ed. Patricia Williams and Laura Chrisman (New York: Columbia UP, 1994), 133.
8. Himani Bannerji, "Mary Wollstonecraft, Feminism, and Humanism: A Spectrum of Reading," *Mary Wollstonecraft and 200 Years of Feminisms*, ed. Eileen Janes Yeo (New York: Rivers Oram Press, 1997), 223.
9. Audre Lorde, *Sister Outsider* (California: The Crossing Press, 1984), 43.
10. Elsa Barkley Brown as quoted in Mohanty, *Feminism Without Borders*, 201.
11. bell hooks, *Yearning: race, gender and cultural politics* (Toronto: Between The Lines, 1990), 150.
12. hooks, 145.
13. Said, "Orientalism," in Williams and Chrisman, 133.
14 Mohanty, *Feminism Without Borders* , 196.

Beyond Intermarginality:

A Case for Intersectionality

Victoria Marie

Introduction

In contrast to the researcher who is white, Anglo-Saxon, male and Protestant, I am Black, born in the United States, Canadian, Roman Catholic and female. I have been engaged in community development research and evaluation for the past year in a neglected area of Vancouver, British Columbia in Canada. This area is not an ethnic or racial ghetto but an area where poverty is the common denominator among diverse ethnic groups. This research climate calls for me to take a reflexive look at my position as researcher in the examination of points of difference and homogeneity, as well as at issues of inclusion and exclusion. The purpose of this paper is to look at how otherness is perceived and represented, and to look at intersectionality as a framework for examining intermarginal research in which there is an asymmetry of peripheral positions between the researcher and the researched. This work also looks at research in which the researcher is a member of a marginal group, while the research participants are not. This paper is exploratory and aims to stimulate new questions rather than to provide answers.

I begin with a brief exploration of the differences between the self-perception of one designated as other, and the perception of this Other by a member of the dominant group. Next, some of the issues involved in the representation of other(ed) group members are examined. This is followed by a discussion of practices in the academy, which are unselfconsciously exclusionary and discriminatory. These practices can lead to internal conflict for members of marginalised groups working within the academy. Finally, a brief look at intersectionality as a framework for inter- and intra-group research is presented.

The Other Position

Certain statuses we have are innate and others are acquired. Still, these positionings cannot be treated as items that can be added or subtracted from one's identity. Different positions or points of intersection become more significant depending on the context and/or what coalitions are being attempted. According to Ruth Arber, recent literature suggests that the nature of positioning is "something strategic, a coalition, a way of resistance, a precursor of agency." Yet, it is simultaneously, "something relational and contingent, mediated by, and mediating, a criss-crossing of understandings and ways of doing"[1] As a member of 'othered' groups, I notice there is often conflict between how I perceive myself and the perceptions that other people – especially members of the dominant group – may have of me. The following anecdote is used as one example of this conflict.

In 1993, I presented a paper at a Graduate Studies conference in Saskatoon concerning the separation of Black or African American studies from the mainstream social sciences of anthropology and sociology in the study of North American people. During a break in the presentations, one of the sociology professors at the University of Saskatchewan asked me if it was difficult for me to learn a new culture when I started school. I was already familiar with the European Canadian assumption that if one is Black, she or he must be from somewhere other than here—North America. I told him that all my family members were born in the United States. He repeated the question. I asked him what he meant, and he again restated the question. Truly perplexed, I asked in exasperation if he was asking me this because my family liked the New York Yankees instead of the Brooklyn Dodgers. Later on, I realized that because I am African American, he assumed that until I started school, my socialisation had been in a totally separate culture. In reality, I grew up in a working class, racially and ethnically mixed neighbourhood and went to the local Catholic school, where I was the only African American for the first six years that I attended. I watched the same cartoons, wanted the same toys, and had the same aspirations as any other child brought up in downtown Brooklyn in the late 1940s and early 1950s. There was one exception. As the Civil Rights movement moved into full swing and gained coverage in the northern news media, I became painfully aware that certain doors were closed to me. However, this did not mean that I didn't want the opportunity to open and go through those doors.

I relate the story above to introduce two interrelated issues. The first is an illustration of the potential disparity between an individual's perception of their own position, and the reinterpretation of that position by an observer who is differently situated. The second is how easily the voice of one who is 'othered' is ignored or dismissed. For example, the main point of the paper I had presented was that sociological and anthropological studies of, for and by African Americans should not have to be excluded from mainstream sociology and anthropology. It appears that studies of African Americans which are presented in the anthropological or sociological literature deal with some form of social pathology, while studies that deal with non-pathological phenomenon are found in the Black Studies literature. Further, as Juanita Johnson-Bailey suggests, when the poor, under-educated are the focus of the discourse, what is absent in the discussion is the privileged group with whom the disenfranchised are being compared. She states, "[r]esearchers often present data on one group and represent the other group in silent absentia."[2] Absentia representation suggests that the attributes of the absent group are the norm and need not be presented. Thus, the production of the literature itself may contribute to the formation of certain perceptions, which become fixed. For instance, as early as 1903, W.E.B. DuBois wrote:

> They approach me in a half-hesitant sort of way, eye me curiously or compassionately, and then, instead of saying directly, How [sic] does it feel to be a problem? They say, I know an excellent colored man in my town; or, I fought at Mechanicsville; or, Do [sic] not these Southern outrages make your blood boil? At these I smile, or am interested, or reduce the boiling to a simmer, as the occasion may require. To the real question, How [sic] does it feel to be a problem? I answer seldom a word. And yet, being a problem is a strange experience,– peculiar even for one who has never been anything else, save perhaps in babyhood.[3]

More recently, Ann duCille's writing suggests the perception of Black women has changed little since 1903. She states:

> I am alternately pleased, puzzled, perturbed – bewitched, bothered and bewildered – by this, by the alterity that is perpetually thrust upon African American women, by the production of black women as infinitely deconstructable "othered" matter. Why are black women always already Other? I wonder. To myself, of course, I am not Other; to me it is the white women and men so intent on theorizing my difference who are the Other.[4]

(Mis)Representation

Television news reporting is also complicit in contributing to and perpetuating myths of the Other. In Vancouver, persons of African descent are scattered throughout the city. There is no Black ghetto as exists in some large American cities. Less than one percent of the population of Vancouver is of African descent. Yet, one December, a news feature about the Christmas Bureau – an organization that helps poor families during the pre-Christmas season – showed a Black woman and her child waiting in line to be served. My reaction to this was (and I think it was justified): 'how long did they have to wait to get that picture?' What makes this a misrepresentation is that in the Vancouver area there are poor neighbourhoods but these are not ethnically based. Canadians of African descent make up less than one percent of the greater Vancouver's population and are spread thinly throughout metropolitan Vancouver. So, it is either unlikely or very providential that a reporter would capture this Black woman and her child waiting in line.

Sometimes, individual members of categories designated as Other are expected to be the spokespersons for the entire group. This 'on the spot' position happens during interactions with the media, and in social, as well as academic settings. Detine L. Bowers points out that "one person or group cannot represent all people who are African American or all people who are women; however, the public expects univocal oppressed groups, assuming that anyone who fits the general definition functions like all others in that category—a faulty premise."[5] This tactical device renders what is said practically meaningless under the guise of giving voice or the opportunity to speak. It is irresponsible and unfair to ask one person to represent an entire group of persons, who are not connected under an agreed upon mission statement or goal such as those agreed to by members of a voluntary association (club, society, etc.). Even with respect to clubs and organisations, this action is questionable unless someone has been named a representative or spokesperson.

Misrepresentation reinforces stereotypical notions about ethnic and racial minorities. Placing the burden of 'universal' spokesperson on a single member of a group cannot but alienate the individual from others within and outside the group. People thus positioned will experience some degree of personal distress. Further, what the individual says is often meaningless, or at the least ungeneralisable, because he or she has no way of knowing how everyone or even the majority of his or her group thinks. Most importantly, it is another form of misrepresentation, which conveys the idea that 'They all think such and such' and, thus, imposes a false homogeneity on the group.

Conflicting Positions of Minority Groups Within the Academy

Because of the formulaic template through which marginalised persons are perceived, silence, censure, and erasure continue to be painful and potentially spirit-killing issues for minority group members – including those who have been privileged, on the surface, through academic credentialing.[6] The credentialing process itself is complicit in the silencing and erasure of socially subordinated groups. For example, Barbara J. Peters, a white woman who identifies herself as coming from a poor background, relates the futility of trying to find herself in the literature:

> I couldn't find courses about poverty. I didn't read myself in the text. I found myself being taught the sociology of the status quo. When I did read about class struggle, with few exceptions… it was from the "Peace Corps" perspective, those from privilege using their advantages to empower those without, a gift from the patrons of the poor.[7]

She discusses how her search took her outside of mainstream sociology to look at literature by and about women and to find resonances in the "thoughts of persons of color." She states, "My poverty background helped me identify with many of the things they had to say."[8] Peters acknowledges that the things she learned in class broadened her perspective, but states that this wasn't enough to make her feel she belonged or was being heard.[9]

Just as those who are other may not find themselves in the literature, Greg Sarris describes the related pattern by which views from the margins are obscured in the teaching and learning process. He discusses how the concept of critical thinking itself is socially constructed and how it serves as yet another exclusionary device. Intentionally or not, critical thinking is taught as a normalizing device. All that could engender a strong sense critical thinking – that which would challenge given assumptions and enable students and teachers "to see beyond the world views that distort their perception and impede their inability to reason clearly"– has been effectively excluded.[10]

Sarris suggests that "cultural biases influence interpretive acts."[11] Hence, when texts are substituted for experiential knowledge of actual people, the result can only be reified bright ideas. For example, Patricia Hill Collins proposes the idea that texts have been used in place of interaction with persons designated as other. She discusses how the work of Black women writers is used as a substitute for "any sustained social or political relationships with black people" by the institutions of the dominant groups. "This treatment of Black women's texts enables members of privileged groups who cannot deal with actual people who are constructed as different under hierarchical power relations to substitute the idea of difference for conflict-ridden interpersonal contact."[12]

The desire to be accepted and for one's work to be taken seriously by the mainstream may contribute to self-silencing. The quest for acceptance and/or to have a voice is not limited to people of colour. For example, according to Peters, "[s]ometimes the voices of the women of colour saying important and vital things can silence the voices of white women who have shared some of the experiences of being poor, rural, disabled, treated as "less than," and so forth."[13] While this may be true, I suggest the desire to belong to the mainstream also plays a part. For example, after receiving her credentials, and as a member of the racial elite, Peters no longer has to be concerned about being accepted. She has learned the language. Certain factors and experiences cannot be suppressed. Racial minority status is one that can't be masked by language style.

Collins coined the term "outsider-within," at first, to describe "individuals who found themselves in marginal locations between groups of varying power." She later expanded the definition to "describe social locations or border spaces occupied by groups of unequal power."[14] She explains:

> Individuals gain or lose identities as "outsiders within" by their placement in these social locations. Outsider-within spaces are riddled with contradictions. From the perspective of members of dominant

> groups such as the White girls in my high school, individuals like me who occupy outsider-within locations appear to belong, because we possess both the credentials for admittance and the rights of formal membership. … formal citizenship rights do not automatically translate into substantive citizenship rights.[15]

In addition to the outsider within situation, there is what Sarris calls "an insider coming back from the outside."[16] This position includes those who have gone away from the group and expanded their horizons through university education. Sarris refers to himself as "an insider coming back from the outside" in his study of the Kashaya group of Native Americans. He voices his concern that his work could have unintended consequences, such as compromising his Kashaya family members or revealing private information. Sarris states that, "as an ethnographer, I am positioned as both participant and observer (and the observed) of certain cultural practices among my people."[17] He expresses the need to "mediate not only between different purposes regarding the study of American Indian culture and texts but at the same time between different modes of discourse about those different purposes."[18]

Intersectionality: A Tool For Social Accounting

Differences in perception, as well as practices of erasure, silencing and misrepresentation, are factors that are particularly significant to me as a researcher. For example, if I leave my racial and ethnic group status unstated, the default would be assumed. Unfortunately, there are defaults for race and class, namely white and middle-class respectively. In addition, because my work is not with the African (North) American community, I worry about the double bind of being ignored by mainstream research communities because I am African American, and by African American scholars because my work is not with African Americans. So, in trying to find and define my position, I am trying to quell these fears. As Arber suggests, however, positionality is more than stepping into predefined identities because identity "is always slipping, always in the process of becoming."[19]

At every turn, I add layers and layers of complexity. And still – and still – and still, I want to write, there is so much more to say – and less. These intuitive awarenesses of positioning – one of solidity, of concreteness of definitive understanding of who we are and where we are placed; the other of increasing complexity, of fragmentation, of change, of being something more or less than– work together as I struggle to define who it is I am. If I am to define positioning, then I must begin by recognising and explaining both these solidnesses and fragments, these more thans and less thans and just the same as, these choosings and absolute powerlessnesses.[20]

Our position in a stratified society influences what we perceive, the phenomena that attract our attention, and, therefore, the questions we ask. In addition, geographic (as well as other kinds of) difference often determines which groups are considered as minority and the positioned response to that consideration. Johnson-Bailey discusses this in relation to different sections of the United States:

> The group designated as minority varies according to the critical mass in a geographical area. For instance, when educators in Texas talk about minority concerns, the minority in question are Mexicanas(nos), and in Oklahoma they are referring to Native Americans. As a hierarchical society, we rank-order groups according to their alleged contributions and participation in maintaining society.[21]

I suggest Johnson-Bailey's perspective also applies to differences between the United States and Canada, as well as to differences in geographical locations within Canada. For example, there are more reports of racism against people of African descent in Toronto, where there is a larger Black population than there is in Vancouver. In Vancouver, media attention and public discourse on race and racism often centre on South Asians, Asians, and Indigenous peoples. In Quebec, the dominant, mainstream discussions of discrimination and exclusion focus on issues of language, that is, the ability or inability to speak French. The inner-city of Vancouver, known as the Downtown Eastside-Strathcona, is complex and may be somewhat of an anomaly within this schema. Most of the research that I have been involved in has been conducted in this area, which has been called the poorest postal code in Canada. In this case, the residents of the area are 'rank-ordered' by their economic status rather than by ethnicity.

Those who live in the Downtown Eastside are considered lower class and 'no good', while those who live in Strathcona are considered working and lower middle class. Yet, the middle and upper middle class business community is claiming more and more of the Downtown Eastside as part of Strathcona. As a result, the boundaries have become quite blurred. Adding to the complexity of this part of Vancouver is the fact that it is also home to the largest Chinatown in North America after San Francisco. The Downtown Eastside-Strathcona area is composed of those working toward improving the quality of life of the neighbourhood, those who are trying to escape the pain of their lives through substance abuse, and those who have succumbed to apathy. The area is tolerant of people suffering from mental illness; therefore, many of the people with mental illness – who were to go to group homes that were promised but never built – live here. In addition, the provincial government's austere policies have greatly reduced the social safety net, which has resulted in an increase in homelessness. The socio-economic origins of the residents of the neighbourhood are diverse. The Downtown Eastside-Strathcona is also an ethnically diverse locality in which a variety of communities form alliances and work together on some issues, while they split apart on others. It is important to recognize, then, that the ethnic groups living in this area – including Aboriginal, Chinese, Hispanic, and a variety of other communities – are internally diverse and complex. As Kimberle Crenshaw suggests, "ignoring difference within groups contributes to tension among groups…"[22] Group membership and therefore, insider status, is not a clear-cut, discrete entity in this area, but an example of Crenshaw's assertion that, "the organized identity groups in which we find ourselves are in fact coalitions, or at least potential coalitions waiting to be formed."[23]

Most studies deal with a researcher who is a member of the dominant group in society, while fewer involve a researcher with marginal group membership studying his or her own group.[24] I have not come across a study in which a member of one marginal group is doing research with a marginal group of which s/he is not a member. Intersectionality provides a basis for exploring intermarginal research where asymmetry of peripheral locations exists between the researcher and the participants of the research.

Crenshaw defines intersectionality as a research tool which treats race, class, gender and other categories as interconnected, and not as discrete variables that can be added or subtracted from a person's identity or from their experiences. When identity is reconceptualised through an intersectional framework, Crenshaw suggests, researchers are better able to ground the differences among us and to provide deeper analyses of the ways in which these differences may manifest themselves in the formation of group politics.[25]

Dorothe Staunaes proposes an understanding of intersectionality which goes beyond the examination of how multiple oppressions intersect. She argues for a 'majority-inclusive approach' in which "social categories such as ethnicity, gender and age are not perceived as special minority issues."[26] Staunaes clarifies what she means by this as follows:

> I mean a view of ethnicity, gender and age as categories that are not the prerogative of certain actors but rather as categories that are produced, sustained and subverted in relation to one another. Categories are broader issues situated in the relations between actors and between different distributions of power. Social categories do not count only for the Others, the non-powerful and the non-privileged: they also count as conditions for the more privileged and powerful people.[27]

Reconceptualising intersectionality as Staunaes suggests would render all under study visible, including the usually invisible groups/individuals held as the norm against whom all others are compared. It has the potential of revolutionizing what is considered the norm by exposing 'actual' as opposed to 'understood' realities.

Moving beyond difference (with its assumed question, difference from what?) to the conceptual terrain of intersectionality creates new conceptual space. By jettisoning the implicit assumption of a normative center needed for both oppositional difference and reconstructive postmodern tolerance for difference, intersectionality provides a conceptual framework for studying the complexities within historically constructed groups as well as those characterizing relationships among such groups.[28]

The concept of intersectionality as majority-inclusive approach, which moves beyond a preoccupation with 'difference', is especially useful. For example, navigating intermarginality is a continuous personal challenge for me in working in the Downtown Eastside of Vancouver. For example, 11 out of the 13 people who agreed to participate in my dissertation research were from white middle-class families. This research was based on the role of spirituality in recovery from addiction. Our experiences with addiction provided three points of intersection between us: addiction, spirituality and recovery. These points of intersection proved to outweigh other social categories such as race, class, age and gender, and provided the basis for interviewer/ interviewee rapport and trust. This is not to say that the relationships were 'colour- blind' or that class, age, and gender, were ignored. Rather, the points of connection and resonance were more important to both the researcher and the participants than the differences. The mutual goal of the participants and myself was to add to the knowledge base on addiction and recovery.

Conclusion

Judith Stacey suggests that feminist scholars and critical ethnographers "bring to their work an awareness that ethnographic writing is not cultural reportage, but cultural construction".[29] For me, this means acknowledging, and being honest about, the internal tension between self-perception and my understanding of the ways in which I am perceived by others. It also means developing an awareness of the dynamics of being both insider and outsider. It is imperative for researchers on and of the periphery to be vigilant with regard to exclusionary and silencing strategies, including those that originate from self.

My present work and research interests call for a framework that will allow me to analyze and reflect upon my relationship with research participants who are differently marginalized than myself, as well as with participants who are differently privileged. It is my hope that by using an intersectional framework in present and future research, I may be able to show that center and periphery, marginal and mainstream are not static but mutable positions.

Notes

1. Ruth Arber, "Defining Positioning within Politics of Difference: Negotiating Spaces `in between'," *Race Ethnicity and Education* 3.1 (2000): 45-63, 46.
2. Juanita Johnson-Bailey, "Race Matters: The Unspoken Variable in the Teaching-Learning Transaction." *New Directions For Adult and Continuing Education*, no. 93 (2002): 39-49, 41.
3. W.E.B Du Bois, "Double-Consciousness and the Veil," *Social Theory*, ed. Charles C. Lemert (Boulder: Westview, 1993), 178.
4. Ann duCille, "The Occult of True Black Womanhood: Critical Demeanor and Black Feminist Studies," *Signs* 19.31 (1994): 591-629, 591-2.
5. Detine L. Bowers, "When Outsiders Encounter Insiders in Speaking," *Journal of Black Studies* 2.4 (1996), 502.
6. Patricia A. Washington and Betty J. Harris, "Women of Color Standpoints," *National Women's Studies Association Journal*, 13.2 (2001): 80-83, 80.
7. Barbara J. Peters, "Disparate Voices: The Magic Show of Sociology." *American Sociologist* 22.3/4: (1991), 247.
8. Ibid., 247.
9. Ibid., 247.
10. Greg Sarris, *Keeping Slug Woman Alive: A Holistic Approach to American Indian Texts* (Berkeley: U of California P, 1993), 153.
11. Ibid., 152.
12. Patricia Hill Collins, *Fighting Words* in *Contradictions of Modernity* vol. 7, ed. C. Calhoun (Minneapolis: U of Minnesota P, 1980), 55-56.
13. Peters, 250.
14. Collins, 55.
15. Ibid., 5-6.
16. Sarris, 69.
17. Ibid., 174.
18. Ibid., 69.
19. Arber, 60.
20. Ibid., 47.
21. Johnson-Bailey (2002), 40-41.
22. Kimberle Crenshaw, "Mapping the Margins: Intersectionality, Identity Politics, and Violence against Women of Color," *Critical Race Theory*, eds. K. Crenshaw et. al. (NY: The New Press, 1995), 357. Emphasis in original.
23. Crenshaw, 377.
24. Bryan McKinley Brayboy and Donna Deyhle, "Insider-Outsider," *Theory Into Practice* 39.3 (2000): 63-69; Juanita Johnson-Bailey, "The Ties That Bind and the Shackles That Separate," *International Journal of Qualitative Studies in Education* 12.6 (1999):660-71; Valli K. Kanuha, "'Being' Native Versus 'Going Native'," *Social Work* 45.5 (2000):439-47; José E. Limon, "Representation, Ethnicity and the Precursory Ethnography," in *Recapturing Anthropology*, ed. R.G. Fox (Santa Fe: School of American Research Press, 1991), 115-36.
25. Crenshaw, 377.
26. Dorothe Staunaes, "Where Have All the Subjects Gone? Bringing Together the Concepts of Intersectionality and Subjectification," *NORA: Nordic Journal of Women's Studies* 11.2 (2003): 105.
27. Ibid., 105.
28. Collins, 153.
29. Judith Stacey, "Can There Be a Feminist Ethnography?" *Feminism and Social Change*, ed. Heidi Gottfried (Chicago: U of Illinois P, 1996. 88-101), 93.

What Do You Mean By A-O-P?

Personal Pitfalls and Joys of Participating in Anti-Oppressive Social Work Education

Meghan Jezewska

I remember the first time I heard 'anti-oppressive' and how flummoxed the phrase made me feel. An educator came to our student/community activist resource centre in south-eastern Ontario and, for two hours, spoke of and facilitated a discussion on working within our community/ies against racism, ableism, classism, sexism, homophobia, heterosexism, and so on. I then put the phrase away in my filing cabinet, along with a pile of literature about 'unpacking the invisible backpack of privilege'[1] and what it meant to be a white, middle class anti-capitalist activist – though I hadn't yet arrived at the point of questioning the viability/liability of calling myself, a sheltered 20 year-old university student, something as grandiose as activist. Interestingly, at the time I self-identified as white, middle class, straight, and able-bodied and did not feel at all uncomfortable listening to the stories of the queer, South Asian, Black and immigrant voices around me.

Perhaps, I wasn't listening. Definitely, I wasn't listening. I was rubber, and their stories of exclusion and living on the receiving side of ignorance, judgement and hatred bounced off my skin, like a game of dodgeball, but without the pain and without guilt. I knew I was a nice girl, a good girl, a girl who amused people and had smarts.

What I didn't get at the time is that I am Canadian-born as well as White; deaf as well as able-bodied; queer as well as living with a partner of the 'opposite' gender and sex; middle class as well as finding significant barriers to employment; highly privileged and also highly excluded and isolated. What I didn't get at the time is that these seeming binaries in my existence simultaneously buy me a passport to good service in places of business, produce assumptions about my intelligence, garner good faith in my trustworthiness, and secure a certain amount of belonging in a given anglo, white space. Yet, the very same conditions of my existence also lead to palpable discomfort, and both conscious and unconscious exclusion, when I seek to participate as anyone else should – by speaking and hearing and reading in the classroom, at work, in activist spaces, and at home.

My studies over the past two years within the school of social work, which works with an official mandate of 'A-O-P' or anti-oppressive practice, have brought me to these awarenesses of where I am located in this town, on this island, in this province, in this country, on this continent and in this world.

In this educational program, I felt my mind was being manipulated on a daily basis. I felt this in relation to those whose analysis and understanding were leagues more sophisticated and humane than my own, as well as to those who seemed resolutely determined to hold onto the gross history, and often present-day realities, of the institution of social work, which often works in tandem with other institutions of the state to police, regulate, and control marginalised communities and families. Is it really possible to practice the profession of social work – that is, to work the social in an anti-oppressive manner – in a way that acknowledges, respects and maintains the agency of those people who are trying to access an agency's or individual's services? I still do not know. I don't know if I ever will. Some of the people I have met through the course of my studies make me believe it is possible, and that it is happening right now – this practice. Others break my heart, and I leak expectation and hope. In short, the school has served, repeatedly, to give me hope, and then to rip it away. The school's website was beautiful, with statements of anti-oppressive intent and mandate. Then, my first semester seriously challenged any point of holding hope, because of how disability played out in the classroom for educators and students alike – for me and for other students with disabilities alike. It seemed as though we could talk of one issue at a time, and never could they intersect, even as an outside speaker was brought into the classroom to discuss intersectionalities of privileges and oppressions.

We had a week for disability – it was not lost on me that this week was the last in the semester – and it was mostly discussed from a white, middle class perspective. The lack of academic resources was the reason given for such oversights – never mind, then, that Victoria holds multiple communities of disabled folk of multiple identities, any number of whom could have come in to class as past, present and future practitioners themselves. We had a week for First Nations issues: one day, three hours, really. We did not discuss the land that the university has been built upon. We had a feminist of colour week, which of course, along with First Nations week, lumped all the people in the world who aren't descended solely from Europeans into one ball of putty, very conveniently. We had a discussion of race, of the decision made by educators and administrators to give students of colour and Indigenous students priority of placement with Indigenous educators. While, on the one hand, this was an active move towards creating a more equitable, understanding and respectful classroom for marginalised students, there were other ways in which marginality – or questions about privilege, marginality, and identity – were erased and suppressed. For example, within the seemingly white classroom, there was the assumption that all of the faces present were in fact all white faces. By silencing and invisibilising a variety of marginal experiences and histories, this assumption created a very unsafe space for some fellow students. Further, even as we were to reflect upon our own locations and challenge ourselves and our classmates, as well as members of our respective communities, we were pressed to move ahead with coursework that at times seemed hopelessly out of touch with where some of us hoped to be heading, or had been.

Many times I found myself hating the idea of higher learning, and then immediately reminding myself of the privilege I held/still hold in being able to access this higher learning. Many times I loathed myself and my own history. Many times I got annoyed with my own guilt and told myself to 'just shut up.' Many times I thought I lived in my head way too much, and wondered why I couldn't just relax and have a little fun. Many times I felt violently angry toward educators and classmates as it became evident that we weren't all on the same plane, and we didn't all want to be on the same plane. Most of all, I resented the school of social work for offering the promise that it would make up for the fractured learning that so many of us acquired in psychology, women's studies, sociology, political science, social service, anthropology, and many other academic and practical areas of study. I never felt more powerless in my academic experience than I did here. I had expectations of having a voice, individually and collectively, and these expectations sank and sank and sank, to where I am now: just wanting to finish my final unpaid work experience, get my degree and hand it to my mother who has worked her ass off with me for it, and walk away from social work and large scale activism of any sort.

Yet, after two years of these kinds of experiences, I have no regrets – but perhaps to have 'shut up' and listened more, and also to have been more assertive in finding a way to be able to listen in the classroom space, that is, in establishing accommodation.

If only it were a given that it were socially acceptable to take stock of and question how we came to value what we value, and why we work to protect and serve our values as we do.

The gifts that learning in what was (sometimes) a consciously anti-oppressive environment give me have included: the growing ability to listen to experiences outside of my own, and to recognize the trust and respect granted by the speaker in sharing those stories with me; the growing ability to reclaim the violence and hurt in my own experiences and make laughter because of and not only in spite of them; a growing love of displays of 'difficulty' or 'bitterness', especially a respect for those who never have and never will be fully 'domesticated' in terms of suppressing anger and humour for the sake of fitting in and getting ahead; and an acceptance that only I know where my home is for me, and that my home is in this mess of uncertainty and anger and laughter and conscious bonds and efforts and work and play and fractured existence, in the best possible sense.

Notes

1. Peggy McIntosh, "White Privilege: Unpacking the Invisible Knapsack," Available from http://www.utoronto.ca/acc/events/peggy1.htm.

Rhetorics of Force, Violence and Benevolence:

A Response to the Events of A-16

Rachel C. Riedner

During the weekend of April 16th, 2000 (hereafter referred to as A-16), tens of thousands of international protesters gathered in Washington, DC to disrupt the annual meeting of the International Monetary Fund (IMF). The clashes in the streets between protesters and police took place in and around the neighbourhood and campus where I lived and still teach. Because of the mass influx of protesters who vowed to disrupt IMF meetings, the university in which I work cancelled classes, and many students and faculty, warned by the university and the media of street violence, stayed away from campus that weekend. For many writing faculty at my institution, this event of national and international significance that took place in our local public space – the campus, our homes – provided a specific opportunity to think through pedagogical practices that engage public discourses and social ideas.

If, as Henry Giroux argues, the work of educators should be to ascertain "how certain meanings under particular historical conditions become more legitimate as representations of reality and take on the force of common sense assumptions shaping a broader set of discourses and social configurations at work in the dominant social order," then the protests can be seen as a potential site for thinking through pedagogical practices that examine popular discourses and ideas of social justice. These demonstrations also provide an opportunity to critically engage the rhetorics that shape responses to public protests, for example the common sense assumptions that guide our responses to the events of A-16.[1] Common sense, as Stuart Hall argues, is the knowledge that is thought to represent the "traditional wisdom or truth of the ages," but which is actually the product of history.[2] Educators identify the ideas that are said to represent reality at a particular historical moment, what Hall calls the "taken for granted terrain," because this is the knowledge that we must contend with in order to shape new conceptions of the world.[3]

Many educators, including writing faculty at the university where I teach, saw the protests as an occasion to contest and transform the rhetorics through which the policies of supranational organizations are understood. The protests were an event that could move students from what Paulo Freire calls "ingenuous curiosity" to "epistemological curiosity" – from spontaneous interest to "a curiosity that is critical, bold and adventurous."[4] This was an opportunity to engage the links between power and authority, the meaning of citizenship, and the construction of social space resonate in the classroom in the context of a discussion of the policies of supranational organizations.

In the immediate aftermath of A-16, questions about the protests came up in the classroom. On the Tuesday following A-16, I taught an all-female first year composition class at a satellite campus that was not directly affected by the protests. I invited the class to talk about the weekend's events, pointing out that an event of international significance had taken place in DC. Two students in the class had attended the protests and the rest of the class had stayed at home all weekend. The students who had not attended or observed A-16 said that, because of the violent images they had seen on television, they were afraid to go downtown. They described the protesters as violent, particularly the 'people in black', referring to the black bloc participants.[5] However, one student, who had attended the protests, said that she didn't find the protesters frightening. In fact, she felt very safe among them. I told the class a story about a confrontation that had taken place on Sunday, at 21st and G streets, in which protesters were locked down in the centre of the intersection. A police van came in, police officers emptied out of it and attacked the protesters with clubs. The protesters, as I had seen it, did nothing to provoke this attack. How can we understand the police attack? Who was violent, I asked: the protesters or the police? Several students commented that the police must have had good reasons to attack the protesters. Other students commented that the police presence made them feel safe.

Several critical questions came out of this conversation with students. At the protests, why was police action not visible as violence? How is the dominant social order shaped so that we do not recognize the violence of the police? How do common sense assumptions about the police's role as protectors of the peace legitimize violence against protesters? In classroom discussions, how can we identify and discuss violence that is obscured by the state, by international lending institutions, and by rhetorics that support these powerful institutions? These are questions posed to students about authority, power relations, and violence.

In the long term, the protests continue to resonate for me as I think through the rhetorics that legitimized the response of the police, as well as the policies of supranational organizations. How could the classroom sustain the critical opening that the protests provided? The following year, in response to what I perceived as a lack of critical inquiry about the protests, I developed a research-based writing course that investigated IMF and World Bank policies and rhetorics. For one class assignment, I asked my students to compare the IMF and World Bank websites with websites that are critical of the IMF and World Bank. The purpose of this assignment was to ask the students to examine the rhetoric of the IMF and World Bank, as well as the rhetorics of organizations that are critical of these institutions' lending practices, with the objective of situating these rhetorics as part of a historical process that is late capitalism.

All of the students noted that the rhetoric of the IMF/World

Bank websites was simple; these sites promoted the benevolence of the IMF/World Bank, but did not offer much information about IMF and World Bank policies. One student observed that the World Bank websites provided many photographs and drawings but little substance.[6] In contrast, the students observed, websites critical of the IMF/World Bank were detailed in their explanation of policies. The students agreed that the anti-IMF/World Bank websites explained the ideas behind IMF/World Bank policies much better than the IMF/World Bank did themselves.

Giroux suggests that to recognize the force of common sense assumptions, or those ideas we must contend with in order to shape new conceptions of the world, cultural workers must produce pedagogical practices that "engage and challenge" the dominant social order.[7] As Chandra Mohanty points out, classrooms are not "merely sites of instruction. They are also cultural and political sites that represent accommodations and contestations over knowledge by differently empowered social constituencies."[8] This acknowledgement of classrooms as cultural and political spaces is particularly important for writing faculty, who teach within a field that is often practised as skill-based and, in some contexts, is seen as a classroom space which is meant to produce efficient, docile workers and citizen-consumers in a corporate world. Writing classes, as Robert Mcruer argues, are often:

> focused on a fetishized final product, whether it is the final paper, the final grade, or the student body with measurable skills ... corporate elites want to see a return on their investment. Contemporary composition is a highly monitored cultural practice, and those doing the monitoring (on some level, all of us involved) are intent on producing order and efficiency where there was none, and ultimately, on forgetting the messy composing process and the composing bodies that experience it.[9]

Mcruer's work suggests that writing, instead of an institutional practice that reproduces corporate interests, can be a space that provides a critique of the status quo.[10] If we think of writing as a practice of social engagement and critique rather than as practices which simply focus on "demonstrated professional-managerial skills," then writing classes can become spaces in which to engage in an "ongoing critique of both the corporate processes into which we, as students and teachers of composition, are interpellated and the concomitant disciplinary compulsion to produce only disembodied, efficient writers."[11]

In the context of a discussion about IMF and World Bank policies designed to ensure and even protect capitalist accumulation, and the state power used to protect capitalist maximization, how is it possible for students to recognize and discuss policies and discourses that support a dominant social order? Particularly in academic spaces – which, as Mohanty points out, are "contradictory place[s] where knowledges are colonized but also contested" – how can students find a language in which to critique the deliberate effacement of capitalist accumulation, as well as the erasure of imperial, patriarchal, and state violence within the IMF and World Bank's rhetoric?[12] How can pedagogical practices "mak[e] visible the shifts and mystifications of power at a time when global capital reigns supreme?"[13] How can students see capitalism not just as political/economic policies and structures, but as a rhetoric: a way of explaining, accommodating, even normalizing, global capitalism? What is the relationship between capitalist accumulation, colonialism, and patriarchy? What pedagogical questions are at stake in such discussions? What can students learn about critical inquiry and participation in public discourse? What notions of democracy are at stake?

Capitalist Accumulation and Rhetoric

In terms of its economic operations, globalisation is characterized by the accumulation of capital by transnational organizations, the vast expansion of productive networks, and, simultaneously, the reconfiguration of the nation-state as a governmental organization which regulates the flow of commodities and people across national borders while relaxing local protections that might impede the flow of capital. Globalisation is not a new phenomenon. As many scholars have pointed out, it is linked historically and rhetorically to older forms of imperialism.[14] As an economic policy, globalisation works in the interest of capital accumulation – the never ending expansion of capital, beyond and between state and geographical borders, in the interest of continued profit by the bourgeois class. Financial institutions, the nation-state, and industrial powers do not just regulate people and commodities, they attempt to produce people and commodities that ensure capitalist accumulation. Globalisation, therefore, is also a discourse that provides a philosophy and a rhetorical framework in which to justify and explain the privatization of public services, the opening of markets, and the lessening of governmental market restrictions.

The practitioners of globalisation construct a unifying rhetoric, neoliberalism, which serves to protect and defend capitalist accumulation by multinational organizations, as well as to disguise the benefits that capitalism brings to small groups of private interests.[15] Neoliberalism presents itself as universal, inevitable, and beneficial.[16] Neoliberal economic policies of upward redistribution rely upon a "rhetorical separation of the economic from the political and cultural arenas" in order to disguise political and economic goals of "concentrat[ing] power and resources in the hands of tiny elites."[17] Through this self-validating rhetoric, globalisation is presented as both legitimate and desirable, while the authority exercised by the state and supranational organizations in producing and sustaining this construction does not appear to be coercive. As David Harvey argues, "globalisation implies widespread (though often informal, grudging, corrupted, and even superficial) acceptance of certain bourgeois notions of law, of rights, of freedoms, and even of moral claims about goodness and virtue."[18]

The modern state supports capitalist accumulation and justifies its authority by appeal to the law and order that it claims to provide. In *Empire*, Hardt and Negri call this the "right of the police."[19] This right of the police is directed toward preserving social order through police and military repression, as well as through rhetorical force. Police authority is "inscribed in the deployment of prevention, repression, and rhetorical force aimed at the reconstruction of social equilibrium: all this is proper to the activity of the police."[20] The state holds a monopoly over all 'legitimate' violence, and this violence is disguised because it is presented as being in the interest of order and stability. Rhetoric, therefore, is a force and a violence that effectively upholds the authority of the state.

The modern state justifies violence by claiming itself as civilized and by claiming to have done away with direct violence.[21] In the rhetoric of the state, the state's role is to pacify, civilize, domesticate, and rationalize direct violence. During A-16, the state claimed to be preserving law and order, insuring what is called the 'normal' operation of everyday life. In such a rhetorical context, law and order dovetails with state power and its support of capitalist accumulation. This rhetoric is in turn taken up by the media and other cooperating institutions of civil society whose officials themselves benefit from collaboration with the state and with capital.

For example, before, during, and after A-16, the mainstream media characterized the state not only as the protector of peace, but also as the arbitrator of social dissent.[22] Along with media reports, information that was disseminated by a local university directly affected by the protests focused on the 'problem of law and order.' A university president decided to close the university, saying in an official statement to the media that he did not want to shoulder the burden of calling parents to tell them that their children had been killed.[23] His rationale followed from reports of violence during the previous summer in Genoa, Italy, as well as from his reading of the District of Columbia's public plans to construct a fence around the IMF and World Bank headquarters in order to keep out the protesters. The result of these media and university pronouncements was to effectively obscure and de-legitimise any discussion about violence at anti-IMF and World Bank protests. A rhetoric of force worked to construct government violence as being in "the service of right and peace."[24] At the same time, a rhetoric of fear obscured any democratic conversation about the issues that the protesters came to DC to articulate. Thus, media and university administration rhetoric entered into the service of the state and the service of capital. My objective for the next section, therefore, is to offer an example of how I envisioned a writing class that could sustain the critical opening that the protests provided by making rhetoric visible as power.

Classroom Strategies

In the spring of 2002, I developed a research-based writing course entitled, "Researching Women in the Global Economy." My objective in designing this course was to create a space for students to develop a language in which to identify and recognize the policies of late capitalism, as well as the rhetorics of force, fear, and benevolence that surface in state and capitalist discourses. The purpose of the course was to investigate how historical conditions – particularly capitalism and patriarchy – produce representations that take on the force of common sense, and to find critical languages which could provide an alternative discourse.

The class investigated international capitalism, considering how policies of structural adjustment and other policies of the IMF and World Bank impact women. The course focused on women because women represent a general category used by capital, along with other racial, class, and cultural distinctions, to differentiate among workers. Indeed, capitalism, patriarchy, and colonialism must be understood as interlocking systems. Gender, in this system, is interpellated by race, by class, by sexuality and sexual identity, by local custom, by particular and continuing histories of colonialism, and by social position in a globalised economy. As Mohanty argues, "the fact of being women with particular racial, ethnic, cultural, sexual, and geographical histories has everything to do with our definitions and identities as workers."[25]

In response to economic policies directed towards Third World and Indigenous women, our objective was to develop a critique of the rhetorics that the IMF and World Bank utilize as a means of supporting the dominant social order. Broadly, our project was to find language in which to recognize and engage the rhetorics and policies of the IMF and World Bank. This is what Ira Shor calls critical literacy: searching for words that "connect the political and the personal, the public and the private, the global and the local, the economic and the pedagogical, for reinventing our lives and for promoting justice in the place of inequity."[26]

As the title of the course suggests, I decided to employ gender in particular because one of the most powerful critiques against the lending practices of the IMF/World Bank is that these institutions fail to recognize women's contributions to economies, and in fact design policies that have a detrimental social and economic impact on poor women.[27] While the IMF and World Bank claim to aid women, their benevolent rhetoric belies the actual effects of their policies. Accordingly, the course began with the following questions: how are women represented in neoliberal rhetoric? How is women's work represented? What do we see when we begin to notice and account for women's contribution to economic systems and structures?

Classroom readings and discussion focused on the rhetorics of international capitalism and its links to patriarchy. These readings encouraged students to read the intersections between capitalism and gender to uncover where certain connections between economic practices and rhetorics of gender are deliberately left unmade. In the context of a composition classroom, I asked my students to follow the rhetoric: that is, to follow the rhetoric to where gender and economic policies are deliberately separated so that the impact of such policies on women is obscured. What is underneath the rhetoric of benevolence, we asked.

Working with Maria Mies' text, *Patriarchy and Accumulation on a World Scale*, and Cynthia Enloe's *Bananas, Beaches and Bases*, we discussed how the modern state, capitalist interests, and local patriarchal ideologies work together to exploit women. I encouraged my students to follow the rhetorical links between gender, imperialism, and capitalism. These conversations opened up further discussions about the relation between the economic and the rhetorical, leading to an emphasis on what Raymond Williams calls the "indissoluble connections" between language, social activity, and material production.[28] Drawing from feminist analyses of patriarchy, the class discussed how gendered power operates systemically. These analyses reveal that connections and disconnections between men and women are not just the result of individual choices and 'natural' categories, but are perpetuated in the interest of capitalist patriarchy. Our discussions of women were, therefore, framed in the context of patriarchal power, capitalism that uses this patriarchal power to exploit women's labour, and the rhetorics which promote and defend capitalist patriarchy.

To theorize the rhetorical connections between patriarchal ideologies and capitalist economic practices, we discussed the complex interrelations between material production, cultural institutions, social activity, and language.[29] In this context, rhetoric, or a choice of figure, is a symbolic and political choice that activates historical relationships and configures relations of power.[30] Rhetoric links ideologies to material conditions, organizing social processes, economic systems, and political formations. In this sense, rhetoric is shot through with (to use Bakhtin's famous phrase) or overdetermined by (in Williams' use of the word) powerful political, economic, and cultural formations.

As a strategy for reading the overdetermination of rhetoric in capitalism, we looked at feminist authors who emphasize the material and rhetorical aspects of patriarchy. Mies, for example, argues that patriarchy must be understood in the context of capitalism, or what she calls capitalist patriarchy. Mies' work encourages her readers to follow the multiple forms of rhetoric; that is, to pay attention to the links between capitalist structures and patriarchy. In order to see the connection between gender and capitalism, Mies argues, "... it is necessary to look below the surface and to come to a materialist and historical understanding of the interplay of the sexual, the social, and the international divisions of labor."[31] Likewise, in *Bananas, Beaches, and Bases*, a rhetorical analysis which conceptualizes gender in relation to imperial power and the division of labour allows us to shift our perspective and to see how governments use supposedly private relationships to conduct foreign affairs. A feminist analysis which reconceptualises gender in the context of international power provides a strategy of reading and re-imagining feminist politics.

In these shared class readings, students read rhetoric as overdetermined: that is, as constituted by multiple forces and linked to powerful political, economic, and cultural formations. A theoretical emphasis on rhetoric as a "discursive act that … configures material relationship of power and difference," conceptualizes globalisation as a discourse that has material effects on women's lives.[32]

In conjunction with our reading of feminist authors, students who researched IMF and World Bank websites noticed that the World Bank and IMF present themselves as benevolent and generous. These organizations claim that their policies benefit poor women because capitalism benefits "in a trickle down fashion once long-term growth begins."[33] Because of their rhetorical assertion that lending policies are beneficial, organizations such as the World Bank and IMF find no need to respond to criticism that their policies harm poor women. Claims of benevolence situate supranational organizations in a power situation where they do not need to justify or articulate their policies and do not have to respond to criticisms of their policies. In this way, the World Bank and IMF absolve themselves from taking any responsibility for the harm and suffering that their policies directly or indirectly cause.

Benevolence has a complex emotional and social content, and a long history in imperialism. Colonialism has always presented itself through a rhetoric of benevolence: as well-intentioned, and as serving the interests of the colonized. Colonial 'civilizing missions' routinely deployed this language in attempts to obscure colonial violence under the guise of help, aid, and redemption. In colonial rhetoric, as Dawn Rae Davis argues, benevolence functions as a discourse of conquest, "a gesture of 'saving' in the name of liberation."[34]

Benevolence is invoked in the context of globalisation both as a continuation of older imperial rhetoric and as a new form of imperial rhetoric. Rhetorically, it establishes a moral response to perceived suffering or disadvantage, activating social relationships that support and justify capital accumulation and social relationships that are linked to patriarchy. Benevolence, when it is invoked by IMF and World Bank discourses, can be seen as a continuation of this colonial rhetoric. Its effect is to interpolate and translate the larger political, economic, and social objectives of capitalism and imperialism through private, domestic, or individual relationships. This is particularly significant for Third World and Indigenous women who are the objects of IMF and World Bank rhetoric and the exploitative practices that these institutions support. Operating under the pretence of benevolence allows organizations and individuals to claim moral authority, thus giving them rhetorical power. This power and authority are precisely what disguises state, institutional, and corporate violence, and how it protects capitalist accumulation.

To find a language in which to challenge the benevolent rhetoric of the websites, we read Gayatri Spivak's preface to *Imaginary Maps*. In her preface, Spivak argues that she does not advocate an ethics that is based on benevolence because within such a framework, "response [does not] flow from both sides."[35] A benevolence which assumes that direct and complete communication is possible, and that subaltern women can be 'helped' or 'aided', is not an ethical endeavour. Rather, ethics is an understanding that communication is always mediated through cultural and political boundaries. As Spivak argues:

> … ethics is the experience of the impossible. This understanding only sharpens the sense of the crucial and continuing need for collective struggle. For a collective struggle supplemented by the impossibility of full ethical engagement – not in the rationalist sense of "doing the right thing," but in this more familiar sense of the impossibility of "love" in the one-on-one way for each human being – the future is always around the corner, there is no victory, but only victories that are also warnings.[36]

Spivak's work on benevolence provides students with an alternative language in which to think through the IMF and World Bank's rhetoric about women. Rather than seeing Third World, Indigneous, and/or poor women as the recipients of charity or as victims of poverty, students are given a language in which to consider the complex rhetorical conditions in which the IMF and World Bank find it beneficial to construct these women as recipients of benevolence and generosity.

I do not want to claim, however, that this pedagogy of critique always inspires critical thinking about public discourses or ideas of social justice. After this reading on feminist critiques of globalisation, students began an extensive, critical research project on a subject of their choice. They were asked to address a specific example which brought together a discussion of women and rhetoric. Before they began this project, students read Mohanty's essay, "Under Western Eyes," in order to begin their writing by thinking self-consciously about the rhetorics through which they represent non-Western women. The essay foregrounds the problems of writing across cultural difference and the difficulties of writing within the legacy of imperialism and colonialism. These difficulties arise, Mohanty suggests, because Western feminism has looked at non-Western women through its own ideological and rhetorical lenses, and these lenses have been shaped, in part, by the aims of colonialism. As Mohanty observes, in Western feminist discourse, women are sometimes represented as a coherent group, and a homogenous experience of oppression is assumed.[37]

When asked to write several pages describing theorists who will help them to develop their argument, some students wrote statements that reveal the difficulty of integrating the critical intervention that Mohanty's work suggests with the assumptions that shape the dominant social order. One student writes about women in South Africa: "women are expected to succumb to a man's urges whenever he pleases. The man has the power to initiate control of sex and women have no right to say no." This analysis positions Third World women as victims, in need of rescuing by First World feminism. This rhetoric operates as a rhetoric of benevolence, activating social relationships that support and justify capital accumulation. As it does this, it allows First World (white, middle class) women to see the society that they live in as free, fair, and democratic. This vision reinforces the idea that protests against globalisation are disruptive, violent, and undemocratic. The student then moves on to provide an excellent close reading of "Under Western Eyes," arguing that Mohanty works against feminism that "define[s] women alike in terms of victim status."

The disjuncture between the student's presentation of Mohanty's work and her own representation of women reminds me of the limitations to educational practices as well as the possibilities that such practices offer. As Victor Villanueva observes, "here, in the American college composition classroom, where our interchanges with students are relatively short – four or five hours a week, ten to fifteen weeks, perhaps as long as a year or two; here, counterhegemony cannot be easily sold."[38] Villanueva's observations lead me back to the questions with which I began this essay: how do we develop critical practices that – in the short period of time in which we are in contact with students – engage and challenge the dominant social order? How do we sustain the critical openings that events like A16 provide? In her discussion of the protests, Angela Hewett argues that for many students, faculty, and others, it is difficult to see the critical possibilities that the protests provide because of the belief that democracy has already been assured by other means. That is, there is a widespread assumption that we already live in a free and fair society in which the government, police, and civil society work to protect these freedoms. Within this ideological context, it is difficult to see the protests as anything else but "disruptive, illegal, a violation of democratic principles."[39] Likewise, it is difficult for students who see Third World women as victims in need of saving by First World feminism to rethink this homogenous representation of women when it helps to confirm an understanding of the US as a free, fair, and democratic society.

If we see education as "both a struggle for meaning and a struggle over power relations," it becomes a site in which to challenge "dominant normative discourses and representations and the active creation of oppositional analytic and cultural spaces."[40] Local events such as the A-16 protests can be an opportunity for faculty and students to recognize the scope of globalisation and its impact on local communities. We can begin by producing pedagogical practices that examine how the protests are represented within a dominant social order that legitimizes global capitalism, looking with a critical eye at the intersection of networks of power that support capitalist accumulation, at state violence, at ideologies of gender, and at rhetorics of benevolence. As we examine these phenomenon, we must investigate both the differences and connections between old and new forms of imperial domination. While classrooms offer the possibility of counter-hegemonic discourse, they must also contend with rhetorics that are identified as natural, the 'taken for granted terrain' that shapes the dominant social order. What is at stake is democracy: the choices that citizens make collectively, public spheres where there is critical discussion, and a civil society in which education provides a space for critical discourse.

Notes

1. Henry Giroux, "Public Pedagogy as Cultural Politics: Stuart Hall and the 'Crisis' of Culture," *Without Guarantees: In Honour of Stuart Hall*, ed. Paul Gilroy, Lawrence Grossberg, and Angela McRobbie (London: Verso, 2000), 141; See also Stanley Aronowitz and Henry Giroux, eds., *Education Still Under Siege* (Westport, Connecticut: Bergin and Garvey, 1993).
2. Stuart Hall, "Gramsci's Relevance for the Study of Race and Ethnicity," *Stuart Hall: Critical Dialogues in Cultural Studies*, ed. David Morley and Kuan-Hsing Chen (London: Routledge, 1996), 431.
3. Stuart Hall, "Gramsci's Relevance for the Study of Race and Ethnicity," 431.
4. Paulo Freire, *Pedagogy of Freedom: Ethics, Democracy. and Civic Courage* (London: Rowman and Littlefield Publishers, 2000), 38.
5. According to http://www.infoshop.org/blackbloc.html, "a black bloc is a collection of anarchists and anarchist affinity groups that organize together for a particular protest action. The flavor of the blackbloc changes from action to action, but the main goals are to provide solidarity in the face of a repressive police state and to convey an anarchist critique of whatever is being protested that day."
6. Alexis Johnston, Student in class comment.
7. Giroux, "Public Pedagogy as Cultural Politics: Stuart Hall and the 'Crisis' of Culture," 141.
8. Chandra Mohanty, *Feminism Without Borders* (Durham: Duke University Press, 2003), 194.
9. Robert Mcruer, "Composing Bodies; or, De-Composition: Queer Theory, Disability Studies, and Alternative Corporealities," *Journal of Advanced Composition* (2004): 10.
10. For a discussion of market literacies, the knowledges of capitalism that are transmitted in universities, industry, and the state, see Chandra Mohanty's essay "Privatized Citizenship, Corporate Academies, and Feminist Projects," in *Feminism Without Borders*.
11. Mcruer, "Composing Bodies; or, De-Composition: Queer Theory,

Disability Studies, and Alternative Corporealities," 5.
12. Mohanty, *Feminism Without Borders*, 170; for a discussion of universities as institutions in which dominant interests are consolidated, see Danika Brown's essay "Hegemony and the Discourse of the Land Grant Movement: Historicizing the Point of Departure," *Journal of Advanced Composition Studies* 23.2 (Fall 2003): 319-349.
13. Mohanty, *Feminism Without Borders*, 171.
14. However, many of the studies and discourses around globalisation present globalisation as a 'new' phenomenon without asking crucial questions about both the differences and the connections between 'older' and 'newer' forms of imperialism. I would like to thank Proma Tagore for pointing out this important point.
15. For a discussion of neoliberalism in the context of an indigenous insurgency, see *Our Word is Our Weapon: Selected Writings of Subcomandante Marcos*, ed. Juanna Ponce de Leon (New York: Seven Stories Press, 2001).
16. Lisa Duggan, *The Twilight of Equality? Neoliberalism, Cultural Politics, and the Attack on Democracy* (Boston: Beacon Press, 2003), xiii.
17. Duggan, *The Twilight of Equality?*, xiv.
18. Harvey, *Spaces of Hope* (Berkeley: U of California P, 2000), 85.
19. Michael Hardt and Antonio Negri, *Empire* (Cambridge, Massachusetts: Harvard University Press, 2000), 17.
20. Hardt and Negri, *Empire*, 17.
21. Maria Mies, *Patriarchy and Accumulation on a World Scale: Women in the International Division of Labour* (London and New York: Zed Books, 1986), 26.
22. On media responses to state response to IMF/World Bank protests, see Naomi Klein's "Anti-Corporate Movements," n.d. Available from http://www.yorku.ca.socreg/Klein.htm.
23. This statement was made to the media in the fall of 2001 in the aftermath of a summer of violent confrontations between police and protesters in Genoa. One young protester, Carlos Guiliani, was killed by the Italian police.
24. Hardt and Negri, *Empire*, 15.
25. Mohanty, *Feminism Without Borders*, 142.
26. Ira Shor, "What is Critical Literacy," *Critical Literacy In Action: Writing Words, Changing Worlds*, eds. Ira Shor and Caroline Pari (Portsmouth, NH: Boyton/Cook Heineman, 1999), 1.
27. For critiques of gender and the World Bank see Peggy Antrobus, "Gender Implications of the Development Crisis," Paper for the Inaugural Meeting of the Association of Caribbean Economists, *Development in Suspense*, eds. George Beckford and Norman Girvan (1987); Peggy Antrobus, Letter on "The Debt," University of the West Indies, Barbados: Women and Development Unit (1988); "Women's Eyes on the World Bank- U.S," Gender Equity and the World Bank Group: A Post-Beijing Assessment (Washington, DC: Women's Eyes on the World Bank- U.S., 1997); Mutume Gumsai, *Development: Women Demand Participation in World Bank Programs (*Global Information Network: Interpress Service, 2000).
28. Raymond Williams, *Marxism and Literature* (Oxford and New York: Oxford University Press, 1977), 80 and 83.
29. Williams, *Marxism and Literature*, 80 and 83.
30. Susan Jarratt, "Beside Ourselves: Rhetoric and Representation in Postcolonial Feminist Writing," *Journal of Advanced Composition Studies* 18.1 (1998): 58.
31. Mies, *Patriarchy and Accumulation on a World Scale*, 11; See also Cynthia Enloe,

Bananas, Beaches, and Bases: Making Feminist Sense of International Politics (Berkeley, CA: University of California Press, 1989).
32. Jarratt, "Beside Ourselves: Rhetoric and Representation in Postcolonial Feminist Writing," 58.
33. Pamela Sparr, "Feminist Critiques of Structural Adjustment," *Mortgaging Women's Lives: Feminist Critiques of Structural Adjustment*, ed. Pamela Sparr (London: Zed Books, 1994), 15.
34. Dawn Rae Davis, "(Love Is) The Ability of Not Knowing: Feminist Experience of the Impossible in Ethical Singularity." *Hypatia* 17.2 (Spring 2002): 147.
35. Gayatri Spivak, "Introduction" in *Imaginary maps : three stories*, by Mahasweta Devi, translated and introduced by Gayatri Chakravorty Spivak (New York : Routledge, 1995), .xxv.
36. Spivak, " Introduction," xxv.
37. Mohanty, *Feminism Without Borders*, 21.
38. Victor Villaneva, Jr., "Considerations for American Freireistas." *The Politics of Writing Instruction*, eds. Richard Bullock and John Trimbur (Portsmouth, NH: Boynton/Cook Publishers, 1991), 251.
39. Angela Hewett, "Whose Streets? Our Streets!," Paper Presented at the Conference on College Composition and Communication, March 2002.
40. Mohanty, *Feminism Without Borders*, 196.

Living in the 'Borderlands':

An Autobiographical Account of How Racialised Youth Negotiate 'Home' and 'School' Cultures

Shaunga Tagore

I recently took a course on 'Women and Education', and throughout this course, many of us were involved in a great deal of 'unlearning' of the very things we were taught during our educational upbringings. This is largely because what the mainstream public school system in Canada teaches as 'knowledge' is rooted in sexist, racist, classist, and colonial ways of knowing and being. For example, I remember doing a unit on 'multiculturalism' in grade nine social studies. As part of that unit, we were taught that Canada was a happy, equal, multicultural society: an exemplary 'mosaic' of cultures. There was absolutely no mention of racism, how racism works in Canadian society, or how Canadian society was built upon racism – even though it may have been the most ideal unit in which to discuss these issues. Through this and other courses, I have begun to recognise how many of my views have been shaped by a culture and educational curriculum rooted in denials of the gendered, racial, and class inequities that exist in our society. We don't learn, least of all in school, the fundamental ways in which women and other minorities are constantly being subordinated and marginalized all the time. This educational curriculum presents itself as neutral, objective and apolitical. Yet, teaching such 'apoliticism' in schools – that is, denying that there is any inequality when it comes to race, class or gender – says a lot about what kinds of politics are allowed to be hidden, and about how social injustices are perpetuated or allowed to continue. By learning how to be a 'proper citizen', as mainstream education instructs us all to be, I myself was taught to deny, ignore and devalue who I was/am as a woman, and as a woman of colour. More recently, through studying Women's Studies, I have been taught to see these things that I was not meant to see. This process of 'unlearning' has allowed me to look back on my experiences, and in a sense, to remember them differently. This essay focuses on some of my past experiences with regards to school/education, keeping in mind how those experiences have been shaped by who I am as a woman of colour.

My parents and sister immigrated to Canada from India before I was born, which greatly shaped and reflected the kind of education I had and my attitude toward education in general. Getting not just good grades but great grades, or being at 'the top of my class': these were always, according to my parents, to be my number one priorities. While growing up, I didn't understand their extreme strictness regarding school and education, but I think it actually has a lot to do with being part of an immigrant family and the issues that come along with that. In many ways, this extreme focus on education may be ways that my parents/family respond to racism/classism. Immigrants and racialised people are often depicted through stereotypes that paint them as uneducated, ignorant, and fit only for certain kinds of work – work that is often devalued within this society. By ensuring that, at whatever cost, their children have access to the best possible education, the best possible jobs, and therefore, the best possible life, people like my parents may feel as though this is one way they can resist the stereotypes and racism they have experienced here in Canada. In fact, many Indian youth whom I know, and who are also children of immigrants, face similar types of bewilderment and frustration around their parents' pressure to succeed academically. I think that many immigrant parents, because they are so protective of their children – wanting them to lead a life without the same hardships that they themselves might have faced, due to such things like racism – often do not discuss these reasons for their pressure or strictness with their children when it comes to education. Consequently, it may sometimes be complicated for parents and children in racialised communities to understand each other's perceptions and individual experiences.

I believe that many children of immigrants struggle, as I have, in dealing with assimilation into the dominant white culture of mainstream educational systems and maintaining connections with the culture that our parents come from. For example, I grew up in a small, rural Canadian town, where my family was only one of two or three South Asian families in the whole city. I probably knew the Bengali language (the language of my parents) at a very early age, but I lost most of it at an early age as well, probably when I first started going to school. I learned that English was the 'norm', English was 'important', and that it would 'get me places'. I was implicitly taught not to care about Bengali or Indian culture, and as I went through elementary, middle school and most of high school, I cared less and less about the culture that my family comes from. I knew that if I actually embraced anything to do with Bengali/Indian culture, people would think it was weird, or funny, or amusing, or at best, 'exotic'. In my last year of high school, however, my family moved to Winnipeg, where there is a much larger Bengali community and quite a few Bengali children around my age. I grew close to all of them very quickly and began to realize what a loss it was to grow up learning that a big part of who I am didn't matter. Ironically, however, when I am around these people, I often face tension and uncomfortability for not knowing the Bengali language as well as they do; sometimes, I do not feel as intelligent, or that I do not 'pick up on things' as well as others my age. What is not recognized is the large role having a community that speaks the language plays on individuals actually being able to learn and retain the language. The assimilation into dominant white culture that I faced all throughout growing up has had other consequences on my life; for example, it has at times produced tensions between my parents and myself. I noticed this tension especially when I was 19 and traveled to India for the first time with my parents. I felt a very real discomfort and was aware of the ways I had assimilated into Canadian culture. These frictional feelings made me believe that I really didn't belong in India, and would never be able to find a way to belong there. This is something I continue to struggle with today, because I would very much like to visit again, but I have no idea who the person I was, who visited in the first place, and I don't know who the person I would be if I were to visit again. Paradoxically, however, growing up as a racialised girl in Canada and in a predominantly white public school culture, I also experience various, though different, feelings of unbelonging 'here' as I do 'there'.

In thinking about this experience of dealing with and negotiating the challenges associated with growing up with two distinctly 'different cultures', I found that bell hooks' article, "Keeping Close to Home: Class and Education," was helpful. hooks discusses the importance of connecting 'home' with 'school', when these two things are constructed as completely oppositional and separate spaces. She states: "Maintaining connections with family and community across class boundaries demands more than just summary recall of where one's roots are, where one comes from. It requires knowing, naming and being ever-mindful of those aspects of one's past that have enabled and do enable one's self-development in the present, that sustain, support, that en-rich."[1] This is helpful for me to think about, and may also be helpful to other racialised youth; hooks' words address some of the dilemmas we may have about maintaining connections with our cultures and families. This writing itself is useful for me, because it allows me to go through a process of naming and being mindful of the effects growing up in a predominantly white community/school, and to understand some of the things that I may have previously been internalizing. For example, instead of thinking that I naturally don't/can't/should belong to certain places, or that I am naturally less intelligent than others for not knowing certain things, I am able to try and make sense of where these notions might come from. Processes of naming and re-calling have also helped me to understand what my particular culture has become, and how that is different from that of my parents, as well as different from most of my peers with whom I grew up and went to school.

The feminist writer, Gloria Anzaldúa, speaks of living in a state of the 'borderlands': "the lifeblood of two worlds merging to form a third country – a border country."[2] As a child of an immigrant family, I feel that this state of the 'borderlands' is often where I reside: neither here, nor there, not quite sure exactly where to belong. I believe that a lot of immigrant families/children live in this state of unbelonging or confusion. Like Anzaldúa, I think it can become a culture in itself. Recently, when I moved to Winnipeg (a much bigger city than the one I grew up in and with a much larger South Asian population), I made instant connections with other South Asian youth living here, most of them born in Canada to parents who had recently immigrated: a wide age range, from 4 to 26. I felt a connection and a closeness with them, even if I didn't recognize at first why that was. I think many of us share similar sorts of experiences and positionings within Canadian culture and society, including the experience of racism. Being together, we also take part in the culture of being 'Indian', but it is a culture that is different than the Indian culture our parents take part in. It is a culture that is strung between both 'here' and 'there', and, in many ways, it is one place that I do find myself at home.

In thinking about all the different implications and effects of what it means for racialised youth to grow up amidst the Canadian school system (and there are definitely more than what is listed in this paper), it makes me wonder whether or not I would be a different person had the schools and system of education I went through been different. It makes me angry, sick and sad to think about how my/our education system is designed, in many ways, to make us all more ignorant. I feel a deep sense of loss with regards to what I could have been taught, or what I could have learned, and what I did learn instead. I feel this sense of loss for myself and also for others around me, as I often notice my friends, peers, or others around me as too 'colour-blind', 'gender-blind', 'class-blind' to be aware or even care about how all of us are involved and take part in power, privilege and marginalization. Perhaps being able to 'not care' is part of privilege itself. I often wonder: How would things be different had I not internalized the racism, assimilation, silence and confusion of where to belong from the beginning stages of my education? How would I have experienced my home, my culture, my family, and my self if I had went to a school and lived in a community that valued a variety of cultures? How would I have experienced and understood my self if I would have been educated in a setting that wasn't so dominantly white? While this process of 'unlearning' evokes a sense of loss, I also feel that it is valuable to reflect upon my experiences and to begin challenging the stereotypes, myths and silences that I have learned while growing up. I think it is important to continue thinking about the rifts between 'home' and 'school' that I experience, to have a better sense and understanding of the culture and experience of my parents, and also to come to a better understanding of how I fit into all of this. Most of all, it is extremely empowering to recognize the 'borderland' culture that I take part in: how it gives me strength, a place to belong, as well as ways to learn and understand who I am and where I come from.

Notes

1. bell hooks, "keeping close to home: class and education," *Talking Back: Thinking Feminist, Thinking Black* (Boston: South End Press, 1989), 79.
2. Gloria Anzaldúa, *Borderlands/La Frontera*, 2nd ed. (San Francisco: Aunt Lute Books, 1999), 3.

Moveable Parts

Olivia Ashbee

Pedagogical Tensions and Ruptures:

A Site for Constituting Identities of Women of Colour Educators in the Academy

Rozmin Jaffer

My scholarship is committed to exploring the ways in which pedagogy constitutes women of color educators' identities/subjectivities within higher education. Along with other scholars, I propose that pedagogical contexts inhabit struggles and tensions of power-knowledge-self. Hence, these contexts are spaces within which educators ascribe meaning to self.

Many radical women of color scholars draw upon conceptions of critical and/or feminist pedagogy. A taken for granted assumption of these pedagogies is that these emancipate the marginalized people of our society. There are, however, reasons for challenging this assumption of critical pedagogies. Hence, in the first part of this paper, I show the way in which radical pedagogies can become another tool of oppression, specifically by drawing on postmodernist conceptions and critiques. The second part of this paper illustrates a pedagogical moment of a woman of color educator in the academy. The third part of this paper discusses the ways in which teaching bodies are inscribed, measured and catalogued in academic spaces. In this way educators are styled and self-styled in order to become a particular kind of a 'teacher' or an 'academic'. Hence, underlying these three parts is the complex relationship between power, self and pedagogy.

Radical Pedagogies as Oppressive: A Postmodern Critique

Theories and ideologies, such as those of radical pedagogies, often present themselves as 'grand recites' or narratives. Hence, these theories "take on their own impetus so that one cannot see reality as 'narrated', but rather the way things are" or as facts.[1] In this way, grand narratives become 'truth' that must be adhered to by all, rather than merely a narrative based on a social and historical context competing with many other narratives. Spivak gestures towards a way to interrogate this 'truth making' of radical pedagogies. The notion of 'truth' misguides us down the slippery slope of setting standards that deem all other social narratives as 'different and inferior'. A particular 'truth' begins to take hold in society as a 'Universal Truth'. Consequently, 'truth' is not seen as a product of human societies but rather as something that exists independent of human societies. This is a modernist conception of 'truth'. Research shows that many educational texts come from this modernist understanding of knowledge.[2] Gayatri Spivak and other theorists problematise this notion of knowledge as the 'universal truth'.[3] A truth declared by radical pedagogies, such as critical and feminist pedagogy, is that they 'empower' individuals. However, we must tread these waters lightly and carefully. Even those who seek to empower can show oppressive tendencies.[4] This is illustrated by research that sheds new light on how these pedagogies can contribute to dominance in spite of their liberatory intentions.[5] Hence we need to find ways to interrogate these emancipatory theories. One such way is to negate the notion of 'knowledge' as 'objective' and/or 'neutral' but rather acknowledge that it is immersed in societal and historical context and self-interest.[6] Another aspect of these theories that must be challenged is that they tend to focus on individual 'skills', 'abilities', and 'empowerment', as opposed to looking at changing the oppressive societal conditions that we inhabit. This emphasis on the individual deters from addressing the structures of broader oppressive societal conditions. Postmodernists suggest that there is a growing need for us to understand the way in which social and historical conditions not only effect but constitute people's identities/subjectivities.[7] Consequently, rather than holding individuals responsible for their oppressed conditions, the oppressive nature of their social contexts needs to be understood.[8] Furthermore, the way in which society functions and regulates to maintain specific oppressive practices need to be examined.[9] Postmodernist analysis gives us a way to understand how social conditions, including language, construct and constitute persons and societies.[10] Moreover, relations of power are viewed as circulating in all human interactions.[11] Hence, power is seen as dispersed and relational rather than merely imposed from above.[12] Thus, poststructuralism gives us a notion of power that is highly complicated, relational and contextual.

In postmodernist understandings, the classroom becomes a site of struggle for making social meaning.[13] The universalizing tendency of critical pedagogy and the right of the 'liberatory' teacher to know the 'truth' about democratic practices can fail to take into account the play of privilege and oppression within any particular learning context.[14] This, in turn, could work against any emancipatory tendencies.[15]

A poststructuralist reading interrogates the notion of the 'liberatory teaching' and re-visions this teacher as one who acknowledges her/his own oppressive relations in the classroom and works with the students to undermine and shift relations of power in ways that open up spaces for competing discourses to surface.[16] Recognizing and acknowledging the contradictions present in the learning environments, that arise from the multiple subjectivities within which we all live our lives, makes it possible to challenge and shift dominating relations of power and develop new knowledge and understandings.[17]

The classroom is a site for these complex interactions of power.[18] These interactions are woven through the often contradictory and competing representations of power around gender, class and race as well as able-bodiedness, sexual orientation and body size, woven within individual's conscious and unconscious motivations and behaviors. To work within these realities requires us to recognize and analyze power as multiple and shifting convergences in particular sites, rather than as fixed and immutable. Universalizing conceptions of critical theories with respect to structures of power and oppression may not be enough to shed light on the complex relations of power that is present in the classroom. Elizabeth Ellsworth illustrates this complexity when she states that in her classroom 'students of color' did not have a unified understanding of racism or their role in effecting it. Rather, there were hierarchies within the 'minority' group that were not accounted for.[19] In the spirit of better understanding pedagogical moments that illustrate difference, we turn to border pedagogies. I attempt to present some understandings of the relevance of pedagogies that are 'in-between' radical pedagogy and poststructuralist conceptions.

Border Pedagogies

Henry Giroux introduces the term "border pedagogies" which offers us a way of viewing critical pedagogy as emancipatory yet 'suspicious' of its own assumptions of power and knowledge. He writes:

> In short, the notion of border pedagogy presupposes not merely an acknowledgment of the shifting borders that both undermine and re-territorialize different configurations of power and knowledge, it also links the notion of pedagogy a more substantive struggle for a democratic society.[20]

Border pedagogy takes into account the postmodern understanding of the various positions one can take whilst interpreting a text, for instance. Hence, instead of only having the dominant universalizing interpretation, we now have a variety of interpretations/narratives from the margins of society to choose from. As students of critical pedagogy take on multiple positions, they learn to interpret a text from a variety of subject positions. Therefore, subject position is not seen as just one but rather a number of differing positions one takes while responding to a text.[21]

Roxanna Ng[22] gives us examples of this through her experience of teaching. The various subject positions she takes on is an effort to relate to a feminist, anti-racist curriculum that is undermined by her own understanding of postmodernism. Ng takes on a variety of subject positions in the classroom and yet none of these positions are 'once and for all' and all are vulnerable and unstable. For instance, she adopts an essentialist subject position as she identifies with 'women of color' and yet she undermines this as she suggests that racist practices are reinforced in practices of naming 'women of color'. Each position is partially released to make room for another, depending on the questions and remarks towards her from her students.[23] In this way, subject positions taken on by educators within pedagogy are vulnerable and partial.

Deconstruction is one such tool of postmodernism that assists in better understanding the epistemology of critical pedagogy. Patti Lather suggests that:

> [t]he goal of deconstruction is neither unitary wholeness nor dialectical resolution. The goal is to keep things in process, to disrupt, to keep the system in play, to set up procedures to continuously demystify the realities we create, to fight the tendency for our categories to congeal. Deconstruction foregrounds the lack of innocence in any discourse by looking at the textual staging of knowledge; the constitutive affect our uses of language. As the postmodern equivalent of the dialectic, deconstruction provides a corrective moment, a safeguard against dogmatism, a continual displacement.[24]

Disruption and displacement achieved by deconstruction "multiplies the levels of knowing and doing upon which resistance can act."[25] These deepen our understanding of the values invested in this epistemology and ways in which we, as educators, may act. It is essential to become aware of the ways in which 'truth' is told, disrupted and displaced depending on the interests of subjects. How do educators take up, respond to and negotiate various 'truths' circulating in the classroom?

As other radical scholars, it is important for Lather to rescue social action in the midst of postmodern deconstruction of critical pedagogy. She states that the way to social action is in salvaging what she refers to as praxis: "For those committed to using the present to construct that which works against the relation of dominance, interventions in the arenas of research and pedagogy can illuminate the intersection of postmodernism and emancipatory projects."[26] In Gregory Ulmer's words: "Theoretical fictions organized into a pedagogy that would collapse the distinction separating teaching, research, and art might also have the power to guide transformation of the lived social world."[27] He poses that the juxtaposition of "theoretic fictions" and "praxis," the central category of Marxist thought, suggests ways in which cultural Marxism and postmodernism both "parallel and interrupt one another." This gives us a way to speak of theoretic fictions organized into pedagogy which may effect social change. Consequently we may want to "salvage praxis in a way that denies both teleological Marxism and postmodernism of cynicism.[28] It is a way to recover the ability to act within the postmodernist discourse. This in itself is quite important to my own work where many educators in my research may, to some extent or another, feel that the ability to act is essential within their poststructuralist practice. How will the educators in my study retain social action within their practice? How will many of the educators who participate in my study see themselves practicing these so-called 'in-between' pedagogies?[29] As we will see, educators such as Archana are required to negotiate various modernist and poststructuralist discourses.

How will efforts of radical women of color educators to liberate perpetuate the relations of dominance? Spivak suggests that scrutinizing one's own practice disrupts the 'impulse to narrate' such that the narration is continuous and coherent, and further undermines our own fixidities of 'truth telling'.[30] In this way, we constantly undermine notions of teacher, student, knowledge production and subjectivity within pedagogical processes.

Postmodernist thought and practice cannot replace modernist thought and practice.[31] Rather, postmodernist framework can be utilized as a tool to interrogate and disrupt specific coherent and totalizing 'grand' narratives of both modern and post-modern eras.[32]

Archana's Narrative

I would now like to draw your attention to an example of how pedagogy, power and self are woven together in complex, ever changing relationships. Archana describes a pedagogical moment in her English undergraduate classroom in a university in Canada:

> How does one deal with identity when it is not merely theory but reality? This is a question that haunts me as I try to deal with the practice of being a first time instructor, perceived as essentially raced, alongside my long held theoretical beliefs against essentialisms, even strategic ones. What happens to the body of theory when the body of the instructor (or the bodies of the students) stubbornly stands in the way of her being able to blithely dismiss all essentialist categories as immaterial? What does one do when a student says in class that as a black woman she personally feels offended by J. Conrad's *Heart of Darkness*? When a male student responds that he can see beyond the racism to the artistic merit? Where does the instructor's responsibility lie? To whom does she owe her allegiance…and what are the grounds for such allegiances? And how should she articulate her response? How is it possible to legitimate her affiliation to the student of colour in her class without giving in to a nominal essentialism?[33]

Archana identifies herself as a feminist poststructuralist educator. This is evident by her preoccupation with notions of 'essentialism'. She states that she is seen as a "…instructor perceived as essentially raced, alongside my long held theoretical beliefs against essentialisms, even strategic ones." Given that Archana adopts a feminist poststructuralist framework to understand relationships in her classroom, she is asking: what ought her gestures and attitudes to be as she practices poststructurally? How does she negotiate these understandings with other understandings that her students may hold? For instance, how should she respond to the woman in her class who is offended by *Heart of Darkness*? How was this particular text chosen? Was it prescribed by the academic institution? What other texts and beliefs are prescribed by the institution in which Archana teaches? How do particular texts position her and the students?

How is she positioned by, and how should she respond to, the white male in the classroom who maintains that one must see the artistic merit of a text even if it is racist? This discourse of 'artistic merit' is common in academia with respect to works of literature. It is interesting to note that the discourse of artistic merit is an abstract, universalizing one, whereas the woman who feels personally offended by Conrad's text is stating a particular reader's response. How does Archana negotiate these two discourses? She asks how ought she articulate her responses to these differing discourses. In other words, how does she practice poststructurally? Who will she be/become in that moment?

It appears that Archana is caught in tensions and contradictions; she feels that she has to make a judgment call of 'who she can be' in this instance. How will she be intelligible as 'teacher' to students in her classroom? She states, "Where does the instructor's responsibility lie? Who does she owe her allegiance to…and what are the grounds for such allegiances?" This statement indicates that she feels compelled to 'pick a side' between the white male and the black woman in her class. How does she justify her allegiances? On the one hand, Archana's poststructuralist utterances may make her intelligible to the white male's comment. She does this by questioning the tendency to essentialise herself as 'woman of color'. On the other hand, Archana becomes recognizable to the black woman as she is positioned as a 'woman of color' given that 'her body stands in the way'. Consequently, the black woman may believe that Archana should form an allegiance with her. Archana may also be swayed to form allegiance with this woman. From Archana's perspective the grounds for such an allegiance may be to consider this woman as an ally within the enterprise of challenging racialised and gendered social practices. Consequently, the sociopolitical category of 'woman of color' may legitimate Archana's own sense of affiliation with the student of color. Hence, this affiliation does not stem from essentialist notions, but rather manifests as a political strategy to organize as a group of women who have similar understandings of race and gender. However, if this woman student did not hold a politicized view of the world, Archana's sense of affiliation would be ambiguous.

In her queries, Archana is seeking to emulate her poststructuralist understandings within her pedagogy. She states how her "body stubbornly stands in the way of blithely dismissing all essentials categories as immaterial." How can she disrupt this? Furthermore, she asks for ways of 'articulating her response'. Michel Foucault[34] would suggest that Archana is attempting to self-style in order to actualize the principles of poststructuralist pedagogy. However, this is proving to be more difficult than she anticipated. How does she "blithely dismiss all essentialist categories as immaterial?" In these statements, Archana is suggesting that she appears unintelligible to herself in the moments when she cannot practice poststructurally. It is clear that she is living the contradictions within pedagogy. Just as for all educators, the pedagogical encounter has become a site of struggle over the kind of self one wants to be.

The questions Archana is asking in this pedagogical moment point towards the experiences of many women of color educators.[35] Archana's questions suggest that a pedagogical encounter/moment is intimately related to one's understanding of self. It is this relationship between pedagogy and the educator's construction of self that is essential to understanding pedagogical moments of difference. A poststructuralist reading and analysis of Archana's narrative gives a starting point for dialogue.

There are several reasons for focusing on the relationship between pedagogy and subjectivity. One such reason is that it allows educators, such as Archana, a way of understanding their own subjectification within the particular context of pedagogy. Secondly, it allows Archana to gain awareness of her own 'becoming' within pedagogy. Thirdly, it allows educators to be attentive to the effects of pedagogy on themselves, rather than just focusing on student outcomes. Fourthly, if we can pay attention to the complex ways in which women of color, such as Archana, are positioned within pedagogy, we may be able to open up pedagogical spaces that fracture and reconstruct practices. Lastly, for women of color educators, how can pedagogy be seen as more than a space where they are racialised and gendered? In other words, how can pedagogy also be a space of resistance and re-visioning?

Questions I pursue in my own work are: How do women of color radical educators understand self within the context of pedagogy? Like Archana, how is their subjectivity constructed and reconstructed within pedagogical moments? How do they employ narratives of resistance to particular discourses and practices? How do they employ narratives of acceptance to other discourses and practices? How do they decide which narratives they resist or accept? How are techniques of power employed to style and self-style these ends?

Rupturing Bodies in Academic Spaces

It is my thesis that particular bodies rupture the current body politics within academic spaces in a number of ways. Bodies of women and people of color, by the sheer fact that they don't belong there, subvert and interrupt the unitary nature of the 'artificial man' of the political body. As gendered and racialised bodies enter academic spaces, they rupture these spaces by the 'difference' their bodies inscribe. In this way, subtle subversive acts are performed continually in academic spaces. Archana's pedagogical encounters illustrate this. Alison Bartlett highlights the way in which female teachers are an unruly and subversive materiality in a classroom. She states:

> A friend of mine tells me that when she was teaching and suddenly

> thought of her nine-month-old baby, her breast milk would sometimes leak visibly onto her professional lecturer's blouse. Can this be possible? Do teachers' breasts leak and their wombs menstruate? What else might women's bodies entail, and how does this affect their pedagogical positions?[36]

Erica McWilliam suggests, "feminist documentations of disorderly, leaky, and malformed pedagogical bodies can work as a redeployment or counter production of culture and knowledge about teaching."[37] 'Disorderliness' may challenge particular professional standards that we adhere to in higher education. In this way, subversive acts can be a productive way of producing different knowledges, such as narratives that oppose 'common sense' narratives of institutionalized academic spaces.

Another example of rupturing bodies may be the pregnant female body. Although pregnancy and motherhood are viewed as normative concepts of heterosexuality and femininity, pregnant bodies in the academy may confound and conflate codes and norms of masculinity: "The significance of the maternal body differs from the public body in that it is the site of the reproduction of the social body."[38] Hence, pregnancy interrupts sexualized norms of the public female body. Furthermore, it confounds our notions of where one body ends and another begins. It interrupts the notion of a single unitary self.[39] The body is not as contained and predictable during pregnancy as norms of society may dictate. Furthermore, those bodies that are even more contested in 'common sense' discourses of femininity and womanhood have further difficulty teaching within academic spaces. For example, queer bodies and/or transgendered bodies also work to interrupt normative discourse of masculinity and femininity. These bodies call into question taken for granted acceptance of heterosexuality, as well as conventional notions of 'men' and 'women'.

Mary Russo's description of grotesque bodies within carnivalesque gives us another site for rupturing bodies. In the mainstream discourse, carnivalesque allows "a redeployment or counter production of culture, knowledge and pleasure."[40] She states, it is this "freakish performative pedagogy"[41] that refuses to become normal. Russo suggests that it is the materiality of the body that is the site of the carnivalesque. The material body is not, however, the "classical body" of modernity – "transcendent and monumental, closed, static, self-contained, symmetrical and sleek."[42] Rather, it is the 'grotesque body' of the carnival, one that is "open, protruding, irregular, secreting, multiple and changing."[43] The carnival body can be viewed as women's bodies or bodies of women of color in academic spaces. Additionally, these bodies exceed the norm in a way that involves serious risk.[44] Women of color educators can be viewed as the 'grotesque body' of the carnival. The more their performances as an academic resist norms of academic spaces, the more open, protruding and grotesque they become. This body can be useful in redeploying culture and knowledge about teaching, such that academic spaces may be reinscribed by these grotesque, leaky bodies. For example, a woman of color academic who calls herself a poststructuralist feminist could be said to have become an uncontrolled, disorderly body that ruptures the present academic space. However, as she does this (consciously and unconsciously), she also re-signifies and re-inscribes this space.

This paper has explored various ways in which teaching bodies become inscribed, marked, regulated and disciplined in academic spaces. These inscriptions are social codes and norms that regulate our performances as 'good' teachers or 'reasonable' citizens. Furthermore, bodies discipline and monitor their own performances. In turn, sites of domination and resistance are produced. Hence, academic spaces are re-inscribed by these sites. New codes and norms are produced. New sites of domination and resistance are produced. In this way, space and bodies become mutually constitutive.

Thus, in opening up some questions about how certain pedagogical tensions and ruptures may be viewed as sites that constitute and re-constitute women of colour and other marginalised educators within the academy, I hope that this paper can facilitate dialogue of the complicated relationship of pedagogy, power and self.

Notes

1. Gayatri Spivak, *The Post-Colonial Critic: Interviews, Strategies, Dialogues* (New York: Routledge, 1990), 30.
2. Gayatri Spivak, *A Critique of Post-Colonial Reason: Toward a History of the Vanishing Present* (Cambridge, Mass. and London: Harvard UP, 1999), Sandra Acker, *Gendered Education* (Philadelphia: Open University Press, 1994).
3. Spivak, 1999; Acker, 1994.
4. H.A. Giroux, *Teachers as Intellectuals: Toward a Critical Pedagogy of Learning* (Massachusetts: Bergin and Garvey, 1998); Jennifer Gore, *The Struggle for Pedagogies* (New York: Routledge, 1993); Patti Lather, *Getting Smart* (New York: Routledge, 1991).
5. Lather, 1991; Elizabeth Ellsworth, *Why doesn't this feel Empowering? Working through the Repressive Myths of Critical Pedagogy, Harvard Educational Review* 59.3 (1989): 297-324.; Gore 1993; Acker, 1994.
6. Lather, 1991; Ellsworth, 1989; Gore, 1993.
7. Lather, 1991, Acker, 1994; Chris Weedon, *Feminist Practice and Poststructuralist Theory*, second edition (UK: Blackwell, 1987).
8. Lather, 1991; Gore, 1993; Ellsworth, 1989.
9. Ellsworth, 1989; Lather, 1991; Weedon, 1997.
10. Ellsworth, 1989; Lather, 1991; Weedon, 1997; Acker, 1994.
11. Weedon, 1997; Paul Robinow, *The Foucault Reader* (New York: Pantheon Books, Routledge, 1984).
12. Weedon, 1997; Robinow, 1984.
13. Ellsworth, 1989.
14. Ibid.
15. Jane Durie, "Emancipatory Education and Classroom Practices: A

Feminist Post-structural Perspective," *Studies in Continuing Education* vol 18.2 (1996):135-46.
16. Ellsworth, 1989.
17. Durie, 1996.
18. Elizabeth Ellsworth, *Teaching Positions: Difference, Pedagogy and the Power of Address* (New York: Teachers College Press, 1997).
19. Ellsworth, 1989.
20. Giroux, 1988.
21. Ibid.
22. Roxanna Ng, Racism, "Sexism and Nation Building in Canada," in *Race Identity and Representation in Education* (New York: Routledge, 1993).
23. Ibid.
24. Lather, 1991, 113.
25. Spivak, 1988.
26. Lather 1991, 11.
27. Gregory Ulmer (1998) as cited in Lather, 27.
28. Lather, 1991, 12.
29. Lather, 1991; Gore, 1993; Giroux, 1988.
30. Spivak, 1999.
31. Robinow, 1984.
32. Robinow, 1984.
33. Archana, 2002.
34. Michel Foucault, "Technologies of the self," in L. Matin, H. Gutman, P. Hutton, P. eds., *Technologies of the self: a seminar with Michel Foucault* (Amherst: University of Massachusetts Press, 1988).
35. Himani Bannerji, *Unsettling Relations: The University as a site of Feminist Struggles* (Toronto: Women's Press, 1991).
36. A. Bartlett, "A passionate subject: Representations of desire in feminist Pedagogy," *Gender and Education* 10.1 (1988):85-92, 87.
37. E. McWilliam, "Laughing within Reason: On Pleasure, Women and Academic Performance," *Working the Ruins: Feminist Poststructuralist Theory and Methods in Education*, eds. E.A. St. Pierre and W.S. Pillows (New York: Routledge, 2000), 173.
38. Rosalyn Diprose, *The Bodies of Women: Ethics, Embodiment, and Sexual Difference* (London: Routledge, 1994), 25.
39. W.S. Pillow, "Exposed Methodology: The Body as a Deconstructive Practice," *Working the Ruins: Feminist Poststructuralist Theory and Methods in Education*, eds. E.A. St. Pierre and W.S. Pillows (New York: Routledge, 2000).
40. M. Russo, *The Female grotesque: Risk, Excess and Modernity* (New York: Routledge, 1994), 62.
41. Ibid., 8.
42. Ibid.
43. Ibid.

Anishnawbemowin dash bimadiziwin

Rhonda Lee McIsaac

boozhoo
weweshinzhigook niin dezhinikaaz
adik niin dodem
saugeen doongibaa

in English you are taught to ignore the first person perspective and to value the objective voice   and in this essay you will find the first person narrative takes centre stage   as it weaves its way through hybridity strategic essentialism   the difference between English and english   and the need to be anishnawbe in a world that wants me to be something else

in anishnawbemowin i am culturally comfortable and at home
in anishnawbemowin i can say
hello
my name
my clan
and where i come from

this i can say to giichimanidoo anywhere but this is not acknowledged in university except where it is politically correct to do so   part of me wants to smile   and nod   and say   how strategically essentialist

i am learning how to speak both ways
both ways i speak
like rita joe i lost my talk[1]
but you do not see me writing about it
and trying to educate the masses
noble woman   this rita joe
the gentle warrior they call her
still sells dreamcatchers in her shop though   sold out

i lost my talk when i was thirteen years old
after years of speaking anishnawbemowin
and living a typical anishnawbekwe existence
13 foster homes in 10 years
what do you mean that this is not a normal childhood
did you not experience this kind of variety   kaa

i knew my mother   my father

i knew the stories my shoomish told me about sasquatch were true
about how to build a good chink with moss and mud
to go between the pieces of wood that he hewed by hand
and lugged through the forest in order to make our home
how to hide the liquor on them when they had too much to drink
how to carry my baby sister over an iron bridge
over rushing rapids down a path into white town
and up past the white picket fence to the social workers place
is this not normal   kaa

since then i have
 – had babies
 – learned my teachings from my elders
 – about how a woman should act
and what to wear
and how to do the special things
that those white women are looking for
 – sweatlodge ceremonies
 – handdrumming
 – talking circles
 – how to build a teepee
 – how to stop drinking because you know you need to be a good role model for your children your family and your people
 – how to smile when people ask you if you are indian cause you sure look chinese to me

talk to me about hybridity will yah   i go to university too   learning how to steal horses so i can become an intellectual   Said[2] would be proud   but many other people who did not get to the ivory tower are also proud   being a role model is hard   mimicking those systems that do not fit into my world view is hard

> Statistics Canada estimates that of the 50 most prominent aboriginal languages in Canada, only three will survive past this century: Cree, Inuktitut, and Ojibway. In the 1996 census, about 180,000 Canadians listed an aboriginal language as their 'home language'– that is, the language they most often speak at home. That's less than 25 per cent of the 800,000 who identified themselves as aboriginal.[3]

It is 2005 and this statistic still rattles around in my head as I heard this when I was in grade 9 many moons ago when I was a young squaw but now I am just listing off stereotypes trying to be funny like Thomas King you've heard of him on CBC talking about being an american indian teaching in canada read his books he's famous his writing quality is very oral he is telling stories to the readers he wants us to read it out loud when you listen to him read it he is really telling you a story listen to him

> This one is about Coyote. She was going west. Visiting her relations. That's what she said. You got to watch that one. Tricky one. Full of bad business. No, no, no, no that one says. I'm just visiting. Going to see Raven.
>
> Boy, I says. That's another tricky one.
>
> Coyote comes by my place. She wag her tail. Make them happy noises. Sit on my porch. Look around. With them teeth. With that smile.[4]

now if you read dis story you find you miss words and you sound like you don know good English make bad indian stereotype but he big writer award winner it says he makes me laugh though and this good thing like Martha Stewart say especially in world where everything still in compartments and in its own place

In reading about English and english, the differences make sense, and this paper attempts to show the difference. Writing in English is seen as a gain for the coloniser. English has made itself a vital part of the world economy. English Literature is taught all over the world and is a teaching tool used to educate the masses. Writing in English is profitable and has a wider readership. Publishers can sell books in more places in the world.[5]

And yet, as an act of resistance, many non-English speaking writers are choosing to write in their own languages. Others subvert the language; broken english becomes a dialect, or sometimes a new language in its own right. It becomes a way to make yourself different, or to take pride in one's difference from colonial norms.

In using Anishnawbemowin, I have chosen an identity and have given the Ojibway language a place above the English language. Writing in English and in the MLA format gives me legitimacy. Punctuation may give the reader a feeling of ease and familiarity. Mistakes are easier to find. C's are easier to assign. I fit neatly into a compartment.

"Colonization is envisioned as a rape that defies the indigenous speech with the addition of European" is a statement that encapsulates my essay.[6] Many times I have heard Indigenous professors and elders encourage me to use my language. Writers like Tomson Highway and Ruby Slipperjack are using their respective languages in their writing. Louise Halfe uses her dialect in "Der poop":

> der poop
> forgive me for writing on dis newspaper
> I found it in dad outhouse, saw lines
> dat said you is sorry
> some of my friends say good but
> some of dem say you sorry don't walk
> so I was sitting here dinking that we
> maybe dalk[7]

In the example above, the dialect is noted; here, Halfe coopts english for her own use. The call to use the Aboriginal languages in writing is being answered.

Writers from a variety of backgrounds and traditions are challenging colonialism in the way that they use language. For example, Jamaican writer Michelle Cliff makes us twist our tongues to speak like the character Christopher in her novel, *No Telephone to Heaven*. Reading the scene between Christopher and Brother Josephus exemplifies this mind and tongue twisting language. As readers, we identify with the main character, Clare, and with her English, especially when she is conversing with Harry/Harriet.[8] As a Jamaican Creole woman, Cliff consciously works through issues of language and hybridity.

As an Aboriginal student, I too have to focus on learning English Literature and the forms associated with 'true English'. One day, it will be important for me to learn syllabics again, and how to speak Anishnawbemowin in order to truly understand my elders and their teachings.

Then again, if "[l]anguage [becomes] a test of race," perhaps Aboriginal students, speakers, writers, and linguists should be more concerned about the loss of their languages and begin to work harder to save their chances for a stronger cultural identity.[9] There is a difference between English and english, and within the study of colonialism or in imagining post-/anti-colonial realities, there needs to be a more room made for english. In closing, I say, "Meegwetch. Giigawabamin nagutch" – again, choosing to come home, but noting that, phonetically, my writing of anishnawbemowin is more in the English style than in the style of english.[10]

Notes

1. Rita Joe, "I Lost my Talk," *Native Poetry in Canada. A Contemporary Anthology*, ed. Jeanette C. Armstrong and Lally Grauer (Broadview, 2001), 17.
2. Edward Said, *Culture and Imperialism* (New York: Vintage, 1994).
3. "Losing native languages," *Indian Magazine* (Radio show, host Johnny Yeso, Feb. 7, 1970). http://archives.cbc.ca/400d.asp?id=. Visited June 11, 2004.
4. Thomas King, "The One About Coyote Going West," *one good story, that one* (Toronto: Perennial, 1993), 67-82.
5. Peter Childs and Patrick Williams, *An Introduction to Post-Colonial Theory* (Essex: Pearson. 1997), 194.
6. Marian Aguiar, "Decolonizing the Tongue. Reading Speech and Aphasia in the work of Michelle Cliff," *Literature and Psychology*, March 22 (2001). Available at http://www.encyclopedia.com/html/a1/aphasia.asp.
7. Louise Halfe, "Der poop," *Native Poetry in Canada*, 248.
8. Michelle Cliff, *No Telephone to Heaven* (New York: Plume, 1996), 37; 25-127.
9. Childs and Williams, 193.
10. www.creeculture.ca/e/language/syllabics.html. The Syllabics system was originally devised by James Evans in 1840. Visited June 14, 2004.

An 'Uppity' Memoir and Some 'Cheeky' Tips

On What It Is Like For Me To Be A Woman Of Colour At A University Whose Structure Is Still Predominantly White And Eurocentric In Its Focus

Michelle La Flamme

Written for the panel discussion, "Prophets, Pushers, Buy-Outs and Sell-Ins: Surviving the Master's House," for the 2003 R.A.C.E. (Researchers and Academics of Colour for Equality) event at the University of British Columbia. Originally published in the feminist journal, *thirdspace*, volume 3.1, November 2003. See http://www.thirdspace.ca/articles/laflamm2.htm

"How long have you been in?"

"I was out for seven years and now I am back."

"How is life on the outside?"

"Not bad. A lot of changes. How long have you been in?"

"I don't know anymore but my kids seem much taller."

This is not about the swinging café door à la Fred Wah, this is about the Wall and hitting it hard. The Master's houses are not built with straw. One huff and one puff or several 'SMACKS' will not allow ease of entry within and through these walls. There is no disembodied, invisible, paranormal experience of Otherness that will allow one to permeate this space with ease. I hit the wall time and again.

I feel the SMACK.

It does not recede but the calluses and methods for breaking the fall have allowed my interiority to stay intact.

Let me explain. As a graduate student, I was, for the most part, 'the brown one' in every seminar. This meant that when I addressed issues of power and privilege related to representations of race within a given text, I was met with a number of responses ranging from blank stares from the class, to hostility from the professor who felt holes were being identified in his (usually white male) curriculum, theoretical underpinnings, or worst yet, his person. I never intended to cause disruption but rather felt it to be my duty to speak to the impulse that welled inside me and seemed blatantly obvious regarding the texts' constructions of race. I thought it intellectually astute of me to encourage an examination of the ways in which a text is raced. These days, I am of a mind to think that I should be paid for this kind of advice: Race Consultation or Curriculum Development or something. It costs me intellectually, emotionally and spiritually to harness forty years of living in a racialized body and speak about the trauma. In this classroom setting, my body is called upon in service of being the 'Native Informant' and my view of the way in which race is represented in a text may be radically different than yours.

When studying Toni Morrison and William Faulkner in a graduate seminar, the class looked somewhat surprised when I addressed issues of 'curses' in a number of texts by both authors and the ways in which the notion of the cursed land and the curses of slavery were being played out in the text. This gothic experience I understood well. I fancied this position to be a Morrisonian broadening of limited notions around the singular victimization of the recipient of racism. I boldly declared that the perpetrators of such violence that is normalized in the slaveocracy would "get their day." My presentation seemed to imply that all of those (i.e., my fellow students) influenced by the mechanisms of a slaveocracy would be somehow cursed or damaged in the exchange. It seemed taboo to mention white culture's fetish for Black blood was a relevant subtext in Faulkner's *Light in August*. It shocked my fellow students that I understood the thinking behind a character's need for vigilante killing in Morrison's *Song of Solomon*, or the rage that compelled Joe Christmas to murder Miss Burden in *Light in August*. Like the character of Joe Christmas and the 'Seven days' that we discussed in class, I had become a traitor: the deceptive 'Other' who had somehow been within their midst all the time. Another student explained to me that I talked white but I spoke Black. Interesting. I wondered if I was linked to the textual Malignant Mulatto which can/will overtake at any given moment? We never discussed the word 'race' or 'racism', yet we were dealing with texts which were set in the Southern States and had slaveocracy and/or its aftermath at their centre.

I felt cheated.

SMACK.

In another class I had to endure watching the triumphant ride of the KKK in the film *Birth of a Nation*. Yes, I understood the horror and the gothic aspects in the curriculum material and also within the dynamics of the classroom where I was the embodied representation of post-colonial encounters as a mixed race woman.

SMACK.

Or there was the time I found myself with a few other brown faces in a First Nations literature class. One day, the Professor was openly challenged by the tiny core of Native students. The students said they felt that her perspective was too Eurocentric in its focus and was missing much of the symbolism. Instead of looking at this as an amazing learning opportunity for herself and the students, she became arrogant and suggested that when and *if* a First Nations person appeared with a Ph.D., she would gladly turn over the class to her. We all smouldered at the ways in which this comment was loaded with ramifications of class, power, privilege and the 'r' word. She became defensive and this shut down class discussions. These students had initiated an awareness of the dynamics of race within the classroom. I often wonder how the level of analysis would or could have been developed, given a different instructor, who might have invited a deeper analysis of the title of Thomas King's novel *Green Grass, Running Water*. What would have happened if the conversations outside of the class between me and the Native students on water, the colour green, grass, grass dance and sweet grass were allowed to be included in the class discussion without the white professor feeling threatened?

I felt cheated.

SMACK.

I took Canadian literature in the 1980s and 1990s and never studied a writer of colour. I felt cheated. I challenged the course title, 'Canadian Literature', which did not deal with the multiplicity of writers who are indeed Canadian but are also brown. Slowly, this is changing on campuses across Canada. Here, on the West Coast, efforts by Roy Miki and Fred Wah cannot be underestimated. I was fortunate enough to be on campus at Simon Fraser University when Miki's Canadian Literature class changed to include Canadian writers of colour. It was not a fight or a demonstration - just a strategic adjustment. At the same time, the tenor and tone of *West Coast Line* shifted people's perceptions of Canadian literature in a strategic and forcefuly enduring way. *West Coast Line* started to publish works by emerging Canadian writers who were writers of colour. I fear it will still take some time to include Aboriginal writers as an integral part of Canadian literature, and not something tucked on at the end of the course so the Professor and/or department can get their Politically Correct credit.

SMACK.

The technique of divide and conquer is still firmly in place in curriculum planning and embedded in notions of the Canadian canon. The wall between what is Canadian literature and what is 'Other' literature is still being built. We needed space, a room, a voice or presence on campus (even a hallway would do) – somewhere we could meet. I fought for and planned the first national Writers of Colour Conference ('Writing Thru Race' 1994) with a number of gifted intellectuals and artists. At its base, it was an acknowledgement of the need for writers of colour to be in dialogue in spaces where they/we were the majority and felt safe to discuss issues that concerned them/us. I performed with a spoken word troupe of people of colour in a band called 'Lime Tears' for this event, and it was satisfying and nourishing. It was a blessing to look out into a crowd of academics, writers and other artists (like myself) who were predominantly people of colour from across Canada.

I peered through the crevices in the newest part of the wall at others like me.

Post-'Writing Thru Race' marks another epoch for Canadian writers and academics alike. It forced the issue of the need for a collective space for writers of colour to meet and strategise for the first time ever on a national level. It marked a space that was for, by and about people of colour. We had asked allies to attend the evening sessions only. The conference worked with principles that I am hoping academia will recognize in its monolithic move towards creating breathing space for people of colour within the Master's House. At this event, for the first time in my academic life, I did not feel cheated.

The feeling did not last. Before long, I found myself in a course on films by women of colour and third-world women, particularly on the representation of post-colonial trauma and memory. My body positioned me as the Native informant in this situation despite the problematic alliance between women of colour across the 'worlds' designated as first and third. Even if I did feel an indigeneity that would align me to the issues represented, I was not being paid to enlighten the class by sharing the insider scoop of pain and trauma.

I felt cheated as I watched the plaster in the walls being filled in the spaces that I had sporadically peered through.

Then I found myself in the Feminism/Postmodernism course where we read an essay about the Black experience. We discovered that it was a white woman who had decided to be the expert on the Black experience in this required essay. It made me think deeply about the text in relation to the classroom demographics and my minority position as a woman of colour. It made me think deeply. How had the instructor participated in the recolonisation of my body?

I felt cheated.

SMACK.

Many of the people in the classrooms I have sat in have the privilege of thinking of the process of racialization in theoretical terms. I feel cheated. We also carefully avoid addressing the race configurations on campus, like the women of colour in clerical or janitorial positions, for instance. How about in the classroom? How is the class racialized and what effect does this have on our analysis of texts?

We talk of post-colonialism in literature classes, but the word 'race' is never mentioned. On the last day of the class, several white women claimed that postcolonial theory is too hard for them (white students) to access. I ask how whiteness is a barrier to a reading strategy? I am honestly confused. They talk of the oppressed 'Others' whose experience they cannot access. I remind them of the 17th century Scottish writers or 19th century Victorian writers whose work 'we' seem to have no trouble 'entering' into despite the vast differences between our lived experiences and the experiences that *these* writers detail. How and why and where does race become the insurmountable barrier and who has erected it? What is gained from not trying to scale this wall? I think of men saying that they cannot understand feminism because they are 'just' guys ... but I know this answer evades the deeper issues of history, privilege and complicity. One brave white woman speaks her truth: "It is our investment in whiteness that allows us to remain silent." In this class, *she* had become the Native informant for my entry into understanding a particular construction and position of whiteness.

For me, white women stating that they simply feel guilty blocks a deeper analysis of their investment in actively denying and obscuring discussions of the dynamics of race that we are all implicated in.

Another white woman wants an answer. In this voiced discomfort with postcolonial theory, a deeper level of the ways in which the class is raced surfaces. Why do I sense that white students do not want to access the level of postcolonial theory that would compel them to deal with white guilt and psychic discomfort? Perhaps they cannot tolerate experiencing the implications of a series of questions fundamental to postcolonial reading practices. In the classroom at this moment sits a stark reminder of the privilege of the oppressor. In the process, I am placed in a square box of the subaltern. What does my own brown skin signify within this context, in light of the reading material? In this room the walls are very thin. The Master's House has become a shanty outbuilding and the air is not good. With a defiant grin, I remind them that we are all immigrants unless we are indigenous to North America. The gazes that are returned to me are blank.

The gap widens, the chasm is clear. There is a patch of grass growing between the Master's House and the Plantation/Reservation I am placed in.

I cannot go and casually have a drink with others when I am positioned in the bantustan region of 'The Oppressed Other'. There is not enough air or time or energy for me to unpack their avoidance and discomfort with postcolonial theory, and our uniquely different positions that inform our participation in the racial dynamics of the classroom. We live and read in different skins.

The air is drafty because the plywood used to build this building is cheap. It is the space where I have been housed by virtue of my tongue, history and skin.

Survival skills are needed by the ones who manage to crawl from community, scale these walls and enter these ivory towers. Yes, many of us are 'the ones' who will make it through these hallowed halls for our families and communities. The history of racism and the racism which erupts within the classroom is an added pressure on our backs. An unacknowledged degree in survival skills is needed to deal with such raced experiences in the Master's house. People are amazed that the two Native women I know who are Graduate students at UBC have children. One even got pregnant during the course of the term and dared to bring her child into a Graduate seminar. There is no room for children here. A long narrow tipi is erected just west of the women's center for the Others who choose to mother and obtain degrees ... some are brown, but not all. Many people do not understand the social and cultural encouragement for bearing and raising children that exists in many indigenous communities and communities of colour. For many of us, these obligations to family, clan and community greatly affect our work here even if we become the ones. The children of the next seven generations in our communities are affected by these decisions.

I decide to navigate the walls of the Master's House as the 'brown one' from my family and community. What does it cost to stay in this space? Dr. Michelle Herrera, a mixed race indigenous scholar from

California interviews a few women who have managed to complete terminal degrees in predominantly white spaces. Interviewees, like me, think through and articulate the cost to cope here. We must also wrestle with the cost of remaining silent and being complicit in the erasure of this discussion. How much can we safely reveal while we are still in the Master's House?

I recollect my experience of taking a course on Cannibalism and having the experience of double consumption. One day, I related the fact that when I was on the bus reading a book on cannibalism for a graduate course, people looked askance at me. When a white woman referred to having had a similar bus experience, I reminded her and the class that the suspicion she was likely to receive was quite different than the racialized gaze that reads a brown person reading the *very* same book on the *very* same bus even at the *very* same time for the *very* same course.

I dig my fingers into the side of the wall and hang on ...

I have sat silently as white people casually discussed issues such as violence in residential schools and other forms of systemic violence. I have routinely compartmentalised my feeling self in order to be able to survive in a classroom where other students dissected texts that were about dark Others and our multiple experiences of cultural trauma. It has cost me to simply sit in the classroom and be present. Remember that when I have to play the 'Native Informant', or race the curriculum in my spare time, I feel cheated.

The racialized embodiment, the post-colonial self that is me as a student, researcher, writer and instructor are central aspects of my engagements with these educational experiences.

When I feel zapped by systemic racism (the hidden elecric current in the Master's House), or the innocent omissions or objectifying comments that are thrust in my direction, I feel the need to escape. Unfortunately, my Rapunzelian hair is simply too short to get me out of the tower with ease. So, some form of psychic escape and compartmentalisation is called upon to ease the sting of the wounds I endure from being knocked against the Wall.

My body gets heavier each time it is thrust against this wall.

It is a surreal experience to be in a seminar analysing a novel about cannibalism wherein the South American man is eaten by his white lover. Still, I sit in my chair and face those white faces in class even when I, myself, am embodied as Other. I'm exhausted after every class. Such a racialised scene magnifies the divide when the topic of the course is the racialised subject and I am positioned as the only visible minority in the classroom. Where is Razack's book *Looking White People in the Eye* when I need it? At times, I mute my politicized tongue and bite the insides of my cheeks in order to stay academic, removed and polite. At other times, I envision white sheets, despite the fact that these are my allies and we are all quite polite and sane and sanitised up here where the towers are ivory.

I can manage to stay in the class on women of colour's trauma in film if I compartmentalise. I rehearse the moves beforehand: use upper portion of body, engage brain and let all nervous system excitement/ memory revert to numbness, gloss the eyes and feel nothing, become a cyborg, Spocklike hybrid or, simply put, mummified. Sleepwalking also works in these occasions. It is the same strategy of repose that I adopt when a racist white person goes on and on and on. The eyes gloss and I dissociate in clinical terms from the present numbing experience. Calluses build up in time from the full-bodied encounters with the wall.

Despite the cathartic release in seeing trauma in narrative explained/explored, I ask myself what does coping in this class cost? I know it is clear. What happens in a classroom when we talk about the 'Pocahontas Complex' and we are the only ones with braids and Native blood coursing through our veins? What meaning does this theory have when we leave the class to join a circle of other indigenous people or Canadians of colour?

What happens when we are the objects of the violence and fetishizations that we study in classrooms with instructors who are not equipped to notice the impact? What happens to the mind-body split that we must perform as a matter of course in academia? What happens when we study and write about autobiography from within our own narratives? What happens when the narrative we study is not just an object on a microscope slide but resonates within our lovers, our sisters, friends, cousins, grandmothers and elders' lives and experiences? Where do we put this excess energy that is held in the receptacle of the colonial past and has no place in this academic space? What fills up the vacuum that is created in this enormous act of emptying the self of emotional content and triggers because it is not what is done up here? Discourses of personal narrative, artistic expression of self, or emotional outbursts are not part of the Manichean division that privileges words and language over all else.

What happens when we study Africa since partition and we come from one of those nations? Do we also divide and place borders around our lived experience so we can 'pass'? How does the act of 'passing' a course replicate notions of 'passing' that we have seen in American slave narratives? What of passing through the gates, passing out from the encounters with the wall, the strain on the joints and connective tissues? Permanent whiplash is not conducive to learning. I recall the many occasions of passing (on) the right to talk, in order to pass the course. Do you Cop to cope, pass to pass, sell-out or buy into this Master's House?

I don't have answers, only more questions. I spray paint them in different colours on the walls. Psychic graffiti is cathartic in the working through of this positionality.

I look out the window from within the Master's House. There goes another academic of colour traumatized and numbed by the racial dynamics of this space.

At the R.A.C.E conference one year, I spoke with a group of women of colour who were also academics. In sharing our personal experiences of racialization in the classroom, we concluded that yes, even here and even in the Arts and Humanities, we experience racism. It is in the very structure of the university which is filled with halls of mirrors, trap doors, and long hallways with deadbolts on doors that we will never be given the keys to. The walls of this Master's House were set as a barrier to our advancement through a variety of mechanisms. Navigating this terrain is taxing to students of colour. Dionne Brand refers to the student of colour in *A Map to the Door of No Return* in the following quote: "Yet another is heading straight to the library to crack her head on Kristeva and Spivak before she sits before a committee that will always be present to her as she makes her way grudgingly and insecurely through academia, through life, never sure, always sure that she is not in control."[1] The writers of *Indigenizing the Academy* also detail aspects of the Master's House, in particular, the "academic gatekeepers" and the effects of their power on the lives of indigenous students, researchers and instructors. bell hooks, in *Sisters of the Yam*, also writes about the psychic costs that academics of colour face in higher education. We need such resources to identify the symptoms and the palliative care that is required.

As everyone is rushing aboard the bandwagon and wants to deal with postcolonial angst or textual representations of trauma, I ask myself why. I am not studying race and hybridity as a fad or a means to carve out a niche for my career. My research is informed by my own existence. I have a vested interest in sorting through questions of power and representations of race within texts and films. It is the psychic food from which I can maintain my sense of self and nourishment for all of the people of colour in my family and circle of friends outside of academia. It is not just about the theory of the text, or a set of reading practices, but about much larger questions of self, agency, community and knowledge.

Why do you study us?

Self-centered ethnocentrism is not the sole domain of white people. Even an Asian ally, when asked to compile a list of Canadian visual artists of colour, failed to include any Native or Black artists. When will people of colour engage in dialogue and research that affects multiple communities of colour? When will 'race' enter the classroom and not be presented as a side-bar to the other supposedly 'un-raced' issues of 'pure' textual analysis? When will white people speak to issues of race within the classroom as a point of analysis when they are being overlooked?

Then I won't feel cheated.

The wall is built on bedrock and has so many layers of plaster, varnish, and paint. The contours are hard to navigate.

Even the wallpaper is a deception.

I have the blueprint for a frame of another house. A foundation is an awareness of how the rooms in the Master's House are informed by the power, privilege and problematics of race. This frame is fortified by a critical study of different theories of race and the process of racialization. Such a design will allow us to see through the windows and become more aware of what happens to the raced individual in a 'minority position' within one of these rooms. Maybe then we can see the tipis we erect for Native mothers on the side of the towers and the shanty outbuildings where we house 'specialty' minority literature and their folk.

Before I close this memoir, I have a few suggestions to speed up the building process. I have some tips to offer new students of colour and potential allies. I do not assume that what I have presented here is typical of all raced experiences in academia, only that these insights proceed from my own racialized experience, gaze and particular embodiment in Canada.

Uppity Tips for New Students of Colour

Read anything you can about the experiences that First Nations people and people of colour have had in academia. They are mostly written by people of colour and may give you a hint of what is to come.

Find allies and mentors who are aware of your raced subjectivity and race politics so you do not have to reinvent the wheel.

Find organizations on campus that speak to issues like systemic racism in the academy. If such organizations do not exist, meet with people and start a group.

Search long and hard for a supervisor who understands and appreciates your position, struggles and insights as a person of colour who is also an academic, writer and/or instructor.

Theorizing racial oppression does not preclude one's experience of racial oppression within the classroom.

Find safe and politicized spaces off campus where you can process the racial dynamics that occur in class.

Balance your life and try your best to engage yourself in research that feeds your soul and/or your community.

This university should never become your sole universe.

Explore bookstores and source materials that are outside of academia if you find that those you discover inside academia do not excite or motivate you.

Get insight from artists who have often dealt with contemporary issues around race years before these same issues surface in academia.

Make the program requirements work for you.

Find ways to NOT feel cheated if you choose to stay in the Master's House.

Get kneepads and appropriate head gear to deal with the wall. Better yet, find tools to scale the Master's house and locate a secure place to hide the brick as you dismantle it.

Isolation is a curse.

Spend time with family and friends who are outside of your university life as much as possible.

Compartmentalization and being the Native informant may exhaust you. If you need to do it to cope within the classroom, remember to decompress later.

Remember, you are not alone. Try to see the faces of the children coming behind you. Remember and honour those who have managed to go before you.

Share your edicts and strategies with other people in similar struggles as a practical means of valuing and expressing your experiences and insights into race and academia.

My edict for 2000: "That which was important to me before I enter university should still be important to me once I am inside."

My edict for 2001: "The work needs to fill the spirit in order to keep from draining it."

My edict for 2002: "Never forget, undermine, or obscure the fact that you are in a space that has traditionally denied, silenced, or obscured the written and oral narratives of people of colour."

My edict for 2003: "That which does not feed my soul can destroy me."

My edict for 2004: "Balance and clarity bring wholeness."

My edict for 2005: "Indigenize the Academy."

My edict for 2006: "Complete the terminal degree if you are inspired to do so."

Uppity Tips for Allies

Here are some other tips for my fellow graduate students and Professors, who are not women of colour but genuinely wish to become allies.

Do not use my words or analysis as representative of all people of colour.

Respect the infinite variety of opinions we have and the numerous approaches to the ways in which we are daily raced.

Do not assume my experience of the text is the same as yours. Give my tongue space when we deal with issues of race and representation just as you would give space to someone who mysteriously walked out of the 19th Century and wanted to voice her perspective on gender in Victorian England as represented in Jane Eyre. Remember that my experience of race may provide me with a whole other set of tools with which to decode the racial semiotics of the text. There is rarely a right or wrong reading of a text but rather different depths of analysis that may be based on the skins we live in.

Contextualize your interest in the dark 'Other' and ask yourself some deep questions about what motivates your research into the dark 'Other' (e.g., boredom, exotification of the 'Other', pity, guilt, etc.).

Don't continually say, "Oh ya, I get that, it is like when I go to Richmond" or other spaces where you may be the racial minority for a few hours. Your lived experience may disable you from seeing issues of race in the way that I do. Try to listen rather than to 'be' in my shoes.

Do not use conversations with me as a site to release some of your white Christian guilt. I cannot absolve you from your own sense of historical guilt nor do I believe that this guilt-laden place is constructive.

Talk with other guilt-laden white folks if you need to.

Do not tell me another story of how bad you felt when reading 'tragic mulatto' stories or any number of works in which the dark-skinned person was tortured, humiliated, lynched, or otherwise hurt or killed.

Do not ask me to read your thesis and then tell you everything I think and feel about representations of gender in rap or some such subject. That is called consultation and it has a price tag.

On a similar note, asking me for information about how a text is raced costs me energy and demands emotional compartmentalization. This should be compensated for monetarily or in another fashion that is suitable to the 'informer'.

Do not expect me to acknowledge you in places that are predominantly for people of colour. I may have to be your colleague in the context of the white space of the university setting, but do not assume I am bound by this tenuous association outside of that space.

Please remember that it has cost me a lot to be able to simply sit in the classroom and be present.

Share these tips with other women of colour who are also in Eurocentric campus settings but remember that it may be something they do not wish to discuss with you.

Do not apologize to me after class when you have been racist, I am likely exhausted enough from the initial comment. Deal with your guilt in your own house.

Do not look at the only brown student when you talk of the 'Oppressed Others' in the classroom. Get in touch with your own oppression and speak from that place.

When you do see other brown students on campus do not glide by with a glazed stare of privilege, look through us, or imagine us invisible.

Don't tell me that white women and white people are not oppressed and therefore you cannot understand or enter into discussions of racial oppression. Your investment in whiteness is likely disabling you from developing clarity as to your own oppression. Look deeper. There may be epistemological benefits involved with unpacking your own oppression in a room with other white people.

Do not expect me to be apolitical or uncritical. It is in my blood, history, and nature to speak to these issues.

Ask yourself why you may think it "uppity" or "cheeky" to hear my perspectives on the process of racialization.

Leave my tongue intact.

Notes

1. Dionne Brand, *A Map to the Door of No Return* (Toronto: Anchor Press, 2002), 28.

Additional References

Faulkner, William. *Light in August.* reissued ed. New York: Vintage, 1991.

Green, Rayna. "The Pocahontas Perplex: The Image of Indian Women in American Culture." *The Massachusetts Review* 16 (1975): np.

hooks, bell. *Sisters of the Yam: Black Women and Self-Recovery.* Boston, MA: South End Press, 1993.

King, Thomas. *Green Grass, Running Water.* Vancouver: Bantam Press, 1993.

Morrison, Toni. *Song of Solomon.* reissue ed. New York: Plume, 1987.

Razack, Sherene. *Looking White People in the Eye: Gender, Race, and Culture in Courtrooms and Classrooms.* Toronto: U of T Press, 1998.

ABOUT THE CONTRIBUTORS

Izmer Ahmed contributed the cover painting, "Figure in Broccoli." Izmer was born and grew up in Malaysia. Trained as a painter, he received his B.F.A. from the University of Lethbridge, Alberta, in 1992 and his M.F.A from the University of Victoria in 1996. Izmer taught painting in Malaysia from 1997-2001. He is now a sessional instructor at the UVic Visual Arts Dept., teaching painting and drawing courses, as well as researching on painting and the body.

Olivia Ashbee is an (anti)philosopher poet and artist who is passionate about collectively creating, uncovering, and imagining a more beautiful and just world. A trans-identified queer, Olivia has a BA in Women's Studies and Philosophy and is is currently working toward an MA in Women's Studies at the University of Victoria.

Tara Betts has been anthologized in several collections including essays in *These Hands I Know* (Sarabande Books) and *Contemporary American Women Poets A-Z* (Greenwood Press). Her poetry has been published in *Gathering Ground, Poetry Slam, Bum Rush the Page, ROLE CALL, Women's Studies Quarterly, Essence Magazine* and *Obsidian III*. She now lives, teaches, writes and performs in New York City. Visit www.tarabetts.net to learn more about her work.

njeri-damali (campbell) studies at York University, Toronto.

Chiinuuks is a Nuu-chah-nulth woman from both Tla-o-qui-aht and Checlesaht nations of occupied Vancouver Island. She is a mother raising her daughter Muhwa Ussmaapi. Currently, Chiinuuks is completing her MA in the University of Victoria's Indigenous Governance Program.

jennie duguay is an artist who lives and works in victoria, bc. afraid of movement for many years, jennie is just now waking up to the weight fear creates. she is currently working for and towards change (however eventual) and is beginning to accept the healing properties of movement and 'rememory' (however disguised they may be).

Wil George is from the Tsleil Waututh Nation (Burrard Indian Band). Wil studied Writing at UVic and has been published in various anthologies and literary magazines such as *Gatherings: En'owkin Journal of First North American Peoples* published by Theytus Books in Penticton, BC, and *Without Reservation: Indigenous Erotica* published by Kegedonce Press in Wiarton, Ontario. He is working on his first poetry collection.

Naomi Horii is a recent graduate from the University of Victoria, with a B.Ed. in arts and language arts. Alongside working with tensions between colour, line, shape and form within her own (art)work, she strives to integrate feminisms and colonial/postcolonial awareness in her practice working within education systems to find safe, creative spaces for youth.

Rozmin Jaffer has completed her Doctoral degree in Curriculum, Teaching and Learning. Her research focused on how power, knowledge and subjectivity constitute relationship between women of colour educators' identity and their pedagogy. Her doctoral work entailed observing and conversing with women of colour educators with respect to their pedagogical experiences. She is currently teaching graduate and undergraduate courses at the University of Calgary, Faculty of Education. Her Masters degree was in International Development; hence, she also teaches 'Gender and Development' in the area of Development Studies.

Meghan Jezewska has gladly completed her degree in Social Work. She is still holding internal debates about the politics of her practice and roles in front-line social work at an agency in downtown Victoria, BC, while riding around in the sunshine on her bicycle.

Michelle La Flamme, Dr., is an educator, performer and writer who recently graduated from UBC (May 2006). Her dissertation, "Living, Writing and Staging Racial Hybridity," focuses on the multiple ways in which racial hybridity functions as a signifier in contemporary Canadian literature and drama. Throughout the past fifteen years she has taught courses on representations of race in film, literature and drama in Canada, Amsterdam, Spain and Germany. She has performed and presented at several national conferences and community events. She says: "In my creative writing, performing, teaching and daily embodiment of racial hybridity, I make an effort to challenge racial binaries as I continually seek new paradigms for analyzing and representing the signifying nature of race."

Rhonda Lee McIsaac, Gooseeyes, Caribou clan, is from Northwestern Ontario and completed her BA in English from the University of Victoria. She says that being adopted out as a youth from her community changed her life. Rhonda's family is from Red Lake and Savant Lake and spread across Canada. This experience of being uprooted and searching for something is a theme that reoccurs in her work; her writing stems from her family, her life experiences, traditional teachings from elders and from other people. She says: I enjoy 'stealing horses' from the classroom and making them mine. I just want to say Meegwetch to my family and friends for their support and love through this journey.

Victoria Marie recently completed her doctorate in the Educational Studies Department of the University of British Columbia. She is a community organizer with many years of experience in community development and capacity building. She was a participant and evaluator of Vancouver's Downtown Eastside Community Play, "In the Heart of a City."

Lisa Okada graduated with an Honors degree in Women's Studies from the University of Victoria in 2000. She recently finished her Masters degree in Adult Education at the University of British Columbia and will continue work in the field of community development and family support/services, especially for immigrant and refugee populations.

Rachel C. Riedner is Assistant Professor of University Writing at The George Washington University. Her work on academic labor studies and pedagogy can be found in *minnesota review* and *Workplace*. Her book, *Situated Cultural Rhetorics*, is forthcoming from Lexington Press.

Donyell L. Roseboro graduated from the University of North Carolina at Chapel Hill in May of 1995. As a Teaching Fellow, she completed her degree in secondary social studies education and proceeded to teach at Glenn High School in Kernersville, North Carolina. In May of 1999 she earned a Master's degree in History from Wake Forest University and accepted a teaching position at Parkland High School in Winston Salem, North Carolina. While at Parkland, she also served as a clinical faculty member at Wake Forest University where she assisted in the training of student teachers with their Master's in Education program. Donyell recently completed her Ph.D. in Curriculum and Teaching/Cultural Studies from the University of North Carolina at Greensboro. She is currently an assistant professor of Educational Foundations in the Department of Educational Leadership at Southern Illinois University, Edwardsville. She has presented at several conferences in education and history including a recent presentation at the National Conference on Empowering Teachers in Times of War sponsored by the Center for Anti-Oppressive Education in San Francisco, California. During her seven years teaching, she has been twice recognized by Who's Who in American Teachers.

Rubina Sidhu is a writer, activist and overall critic from Victoria, BC. Her time at the University of Victoria has taught her that there is much more learning to be done than in the classroom. She encourages more women of colour to write and tell stories of histories forgotten or neglected.

Proma Tagore teaches and researches at the University of Victoria in the areas of post/anti-colonial, anti-racist, feminist and queer studies. Her work has been published in venues such as *Journal of Canadian Poetry* (forthcoming); *Five Lenses for Anti-Oppressive Education* (eds. Kumashiro and Ngo, Peter Lang, forthcoming); and *Red Silk: An Anthology of South Asian Canadian Women Poets* (eds. Dunlop and Uppal, Mansfield, 2004). She is currently working on a book-length manuscript, *The Shapes of Silence: Writing by Women of Colour and the Politics of Testimony*. She has been truly lucky to be able to work with some very smart and talented students over the past six years of teaching at UVic. *In Our Own Voices* is dedicated to them.

Shaunga Tagore is a Women's Studies undergraduate student at York University. She is a self-proclaimed singer/songwriter/poet, and music and art have always been a big part of her life. Other interests include: good people, good friends, good entertainment and good humour. She sees her involvements with music, poetry and art as intimately tied to anti-oppressive activism – in ways that are both personal and political.